# The Odyssey of Survival

# The Odyssey of Survival

# The Odyssey

# Of

# Survival

The Odyssey of Survival

## *"The Odyssey of Survival"*

*Republished 2017 by:*

**Lolana Mack Publishing**
Email: lolanamackpublishing@gmail.com
678-631-7349

Cover Design: Janiel Escueta

ISBN
978-0-9977804-1-3

Lolana Mack Publishing: All rights reserved. Without limiting the rights under copyright reserved above, no part of this book may be reproduced, stored in or introduced into a retrieval system, or transmitted, in any form, or by any means (electronic, mechanical, photocopying, recording, or otherwise), without prior written consent from both the author and publisher Lolana Mack Publishing, except brief quotes used in reviews.
©2017 by Lolana Mack Publishing. All rights reserved.
All Scriptures quotations, unless otherwise indicated, are taken from the Amplified version of the Holy Bible.

The Odyssey of Survival

"Fear not, for I am with you; do not be dismayed, for I am your God. I will strengthen you, yes, I will help you, yes, I will uphold you with the right hand of my righteousness."

Isaiah 41: 10 (KJV)

The Odyssey of Survival

## Table of Contents:

    i.  Memory

    ii.  Introduction

    vi.  Acknowledgements

1. The Muddied Head of the Stream
2. Loss
3. Hell on Earth
4. Tragedy of Tragedies
5. Alliance with the Devil
6. Sold for a Fistful of Dollars
7. Betrayals
8. Good & Evil, Truth & Lies
9. Seventeen and Pregnant
10. Survival
11. My First Born
12. Rape and Unconsented Abortion
13. Death of a Child
14. Two New Babies
15. Freedom from Mother
16. Mother's Wrath
17. Homelessness
18. Finding Refuge
19. Dawning of a New Day

The Odyssey of Survival

## *Memory*

I will never forget my beloved Daddy. The hole in my heart for you is deeper than the one in which your soft brown eyes and lips that were always ready with a smile, lay frozen.

I wish I could see you one more time.

I love you.

## *Introduction*

I live pretending to be the product of a normal family. I have formed a web, creating a world of my own, in which I have severed or in many instances distorted the truth of the time following the first twelve years of my life. This was the age of my first rape. The rapist had my mother's permission to do as he wished with me. She was handsomely paid.

These traumatic experiences have left me dysfunctional and paralyzed by fear. I have hidden the truth of my past, conjuring up stories to make me look good in the eyes of others. Discussions about Mothers are always avoided, because I cannot be an enthusiastic participant. I have no glowing, loving, caring pictures of my Mother. My portrait of her is dark, monstrous and menacing. Her arms do not comfort, they hurt. Her lips have never kissed us, they spit in our faces. Her legs don't bring her to our sides, when we cry out in pain; they kick us in our guts.

How can I tell anyone that I hate my Mother?

The pain of abuse seems like it happened yesterday, and the shame of it causes me to keep my mouth closed. How can I talk, and who can I tell these sordid details of a family that has experienced such unimaginable cruelties at the hands of its protector? A series of events, occurring during a six-week period, takes me to a place where I'm suffocating. Daily my soul cries out for release and sleep eludes me at night. Every fiber of my being screams, begging for the shackles in which it has been imprisoned for so long, to be broken. Shame stops me from relating even a portion of my past to anyone. I am afraid of being judged by my friends. I am scared that the few people, who say they love and respect me, will stop caring about me.

# The Odyssey of Survival

I do not want to be talked about behind my back. Nor do I want to be laughed at, scorned and ridiculed by a society that thinks a child is responsible for at least some of the injustices done to them. That's what my mother said, even though she was the one who instigated the abuses against us.

This story has been told to no one. My former husband of twenty years has no inkling of my past. If he had even suspected the truth he would have raced to a divorce lawyer putting distance between us as fast as possible. My present husband of two years is also in the dark. I'm trying to find the courage to enlighten him before production of this book is completed. My family – well, we are all in the same boat, which is about to capsize. We all need help finding wholeness in our lives, and I hope this is a step in the right direction.

My friends – maybe they won't recognize my name on the cover. Maybe I won't tell them I have written a book. That will not work, I talk too much.

O Lord, what are they going to think about me? I have concealed the truth of my past by telling them only about the few good things. The very person, who raped and abused me, is portrayed as the best part of my life. The details have been carefully erased.

But, if I can help one person break the insidious silence on rape and abuse, then the snickers from the ignorant will be well taken.

Everything I have lived and have been told is shrouded in lies and deception. Nothing is, as it seems. The entire family history has never been told. Dark secrets of the past are hidden so deep that no amount of research can possibly unearth all the truth from the abyss in which they have been buried.

Our grandmother, Miss Ruby lived to be ninety-six years old and her life was spent hiding the facts about the fathers of her children and the true history of the family line. Children and grandchildren attended school in names other than their fathers. Names were changed to ensure that secrets remained hidden.

# The Odyssey of Survival

My siblings and I have managed, only by the grace of God, to survive our childhood and early adulthood. Our mother hated us and tried her best to kill us. She pitted us against each other, further alienating the family. Today we manage to be friends with one another. I thank God we have made it.

I believe God was there and spoke to me the night I danced in a nightclub that was blue with cigarette smoke as I held a glass of whiskey in my hand. Four months later He led me to attend a crusade, where He again spoke to me, overshadowing me with His Holy presence. He fought and won the battle with the devil for my soul.

As we embark on this journey together my healing is in progress. At the completion of your journey I would like to hear from you. Please send me your answers and comments to the **Life questions** at the end of each chapter. I would like to know how my journey helped you in your struggles with your own issues.

*Send me your thoughts, questions, ideas, comments and suggestions. I will personally respond to each of you.*

*Marcia Fisher*

**Revamp My Life Ministries, Inc.**
Email: revampmylifeministries@gmail.com
Website: Revampmylifeministries.com
Facebook: Marcia Fisher

## *Acknowledgements*

My deepest and most sincere appreciation goes to God for his everlasting love and saving grace. It is only because He loves us so much, that He gave his life to save the human race, making it possible for sinners like me to have a place in His kingdom.

I am grateful to my supportive and loving family, who has encouraged me in the painful and tedious task of completing this work. It has been a long journey paved with many tears and misgivings, but here I am, a survivor.

Mother; I have forgiven you for all the injustices you sanctioned and performed against me. You are lying silent in your grave. How I wish for one more opportunity to try and make things right between us.

May God bless you, and I pray that you'll be a part of the first resurrection.

*The names of the characters have been changed to protect the privacy of the persons depicted in this true story of my life.*

# The Odyssey of Survival

## Chapter One

## THE MUDDIED HEAD OF THE STREAM

In a little town called Spring Field, in the parish of St. Elizabeth, Jamaica, W.I., a union is formed between Ruby Lynch and Charles Grant Their union produces seven children. Only three daughters survive infancy. In those days most of the citizens of Jamaica were poor and improvised. There was little money available and few opportunities for a career or entrepreneurship. Food came from working the fields, and meat from the rearing and slaughter of animals. Running water and electricity were unheard of; children did most of the work around the house and in the fields. Adequate medical care was not readily available; the elderly were left to die from preventable ailments, the young suffered from many childhood diseases, and the newborn struggle, often losing the fight before reaching their first birthday.

With the advent of technology our parents never missed an opportunity to tell us how lucky we were to have food on our plates which we did not have to plant, reap or kill, water coming out of a faucet instead of having to go to the river to fetch it, bringing it back on our heads. Flushing toilets in the house was a novelty, and the luxury of the flick of a switch on the wall, getting light – well, they had to catch peeni-wallies in jars using them to light their pathway.

School, if you were lucky enough to be allowed to attend, was miles away from home; the distance was covered twice daily in bare feet. There was no time for play. The animals had to be cared for before dark, supplies to be brought in from the field, water to be fetched, wood to be gathered for the stove, meals to be cooked. The endless chores seemed to begin again as soon as weary heads hit the dry trash-covered pillow.

# The Odyssey of Survival

The Grant's children are deprived of childhood freedom; nurturing and motherly love has never visited their home. Instead, the iron fist of mother remains tightly clenched waiting to strike out at the smallest infraction. Mother rules over them with an iron hand. Their every move is watched. The brief periods spent away from her hawk eyes have to be accounted for to her satisfaction, or a whipping is a sure thing. As the girls grow older mother begin looking for suitable husbands for them. Although this is not the custom of the island, she decides that they can only be married to someone hand picked by her, and there is no argument about it. The three daughters of Ruby and Charles allow sibling rivalry to forge a rift in their relationship, partly caused by jealousy of each other. Why does one have dark skin and kinky hair, one boasts almost white skin with beautiful flowing black curls, while the last child is a beauty with Indian features and long hair cascading down her back. She is called Cinderella. How can three children of the same parentage look and behave so differently? There is no comradeship, no secrets, and no friendship; instead they resent each other. No love is lost between them.

Vira the eldest daughter is sixteen years old. Billy Starcky, a zealous young man comes through the town with a bible tucked under his arm intent on teaching the word of God to the parishioners. He visits each home, giving bible studies to any who will listen. On one of his treks, Billy knocks on the Grant's front door. Reluctantly, Ruby allows him entry into her home. Seated around the dining table, he tries his best to convince her that there is a God who created the world, and who love and cares enough about her to have died on Calvary's cross to save her and the world from their sins. He teaches that God deserves to be acknowledged, praised and served. He is met with great resistance from Ruby about the validity, existence, and goodness of his God.

While trying to quote scripture to prove his point a movement catches his eyes. From his peripheral vision he notices a young lady sitting in a corner of the darkened room.
Miss Ruby is not a religious woman and there was no convincing her that she needs God.

# The Odyssey of Survival

She has been doing quite well without Him and doesn't need Him now to complicate her life with all His rules and "thou shalt nots." She makes the rules in her household and everyone lives by them or faces her judgment. No Sir, she has no need for God.

When he is not trying to convert the neighborhood, Billy can be found in the field. He is a successful farmer from an adjoining community. With only an elementary education he has somehow learned to read the Bible and is able to accurately quote scripture from Genesis to Revelation. Using all his efforts, he persuades Miss Ruby to allow him another visit into her home for Bible study, even though she doesn't feel the need for God. Telling him to stop wasting her time, she leads him to the kitchen table. Quickly he scans the room. Yes, he sees her. During his lesson study his eyes are constantly drifting to the silent figure shrouded in shadows in a corner. Not only has he noticed the young lady's quiet presence, he also notices the slumped shoulders: the unhappy countenance. Never is the slightest a smile shown in the direction of the visiting man of God.

Vira sits quietly in the corner for several reasons. She hates her mother, resents her two sisters, and despises her situation. She had been fortunate enough to be raised in the city (Kingston), with her godparents. Her mother had been sent to Kingston, as a young girl to work as a domestic help in the home of a family; Going about the business of keeping the home clean, preparing meals, and hand washing their laundry. She has no social life. Mrs. Bogle is pleased with her work, and Mr. Bogle is pleased with the way her young body has developed as she budded from a lanky and shy fourteen year old, into a shapely young lady. Hiding behind the newspaper, feigning interest in the reported news, he intently watches her moving about the house, paying special attention to the swaying of her hips. He plots to find a way to be alone with her. Thoughts of how delectable her young body will feel in his arms fill his head. He has to have her.

One fateful day he remains home from work. Standing over the sink washing the family's dirty breakfast dishes, Ruby is oblivious to his presence as he silently approaches her from behind. Her young body stiffens when he spoke. He is too close for comfort. Fear leaps in her heart as she feels his hot breath on the back of her neck. His hands roam over her breast, and his lips whisper forbidden suggestions in her ears.

"Hi pretty girl. You look beautiful this morning."

"Mr. Bogle stop it sir." She pleads.

Ignoring her whimper, he continues.
"I have been watching you for a long time, and have something I want to give to you."

"Sir I am only here to work for you and the missus, please stop it, I don't want to get in any trouble with your wife, she is good to me, please sir, stop it."

Scoffing at her pleas; his hands continue, finding their way down between her legs. She wiggles trying her best to get away, but he is persistent, refusing to abandon his intentions.

She weighs no more than one hundred pounds, and he easily maneuvers her away from the sink to a more comfortable place. Laying her on the couch, he uses his masculine skills to woo her into relenting to his demands. Slowly, carefully, skillfully, he has her in his arms, where he kisses her lips, neck and breasts.

"Don't move around so much, relax it's going to be alright." He croons.

"No sir, Mr. Bogle please stop you are hurting me and the missus is going to be mad if she finds out about this".

"Who's going to tell her, you? He smirks.

"Oh God help me, please sir, please don't."

# The Odyssey of Survival

Before long he eases himself off the couch and is lying on top of her. There he has intercourse with his sixteen-year-old household help. Satisfied, he takes the time to comfort her newly deflowered body.

"You were wonderful, so sweet, it will be better next time, you won't hurt as much, you'll see. But remember, this is our secret, Mrs. Bogle must never know about this, okay, if you tell her I will deny all of it and you will be sent packing back to St. Elizabeth to work the fields and live in poverty. Do you understand me? Not one word out of you to anyone."

Anything is better than being sent back to St. Elizabeth. In St. Elizabeth each day begins before sunrise. The cows, goats, and donkeys have to be taken out to pasture, eggs need to be gathered from the chicken coop, the cows to be milked, fire to be made, getting down on hands and knees, blowing the lit match, hoping the pyramid of wood will catch and burn. She hated her existence there. She has to remain in the city, even if it means being raped by her boss.

Next time is three days later, when instead of leaving at his usual time, he lingers giving his wife an excuse. This time he is met with less resistance. Her soreness has eased and her curiosity has been engaged. When his arms circled her body, and his hot breath brushed her neck, a secret smile plays across her lips, and after a moment's hesitation she leans into his broad chest. Willingly she walks to the couch, allowing him to fondle, caress, and kiss her. When their bodies meet as one she follows his movements, enjoying the culmination of the act. At least twice per week for the following three weeks her household work is interrupted by lust and raw sexual cravings. She has certainly fallen head over heels in love with her boss. He on the other hand has only been enjoying himself with a new distraction. Her world comes crashing down around her, when her monthly cycle doesn't arrive. Sex education has been limited, but she knows enough to recognize the smell of trouble. The stench of doom is in her nostrils when the next month's cycle fails to appear. Concerned, she voices her worry to her lover who tells her that, if that is the case, she will have to find someplace else to go, his home cannot be disrupted, and his wife cannot be made privy to such a matter. "One word from you, and I will deny any involvement with you, and you will be out the door and on a bus back to St. Elizabeth." He warns.

What is she going to do? The worst thing imaginable has happened. Returning home to mother is out of the question. She had been sent to Kingston to earn a livelihood for the family, to lift them out of the trenches. She had been given the opportunity to make a better life for herself. If she returns with a baby in her arms, the child will probably be thrown in the river and she will be ostracized from the family. She needs another solution. Mother has to be kept in the dark. There is one person to whom she can turn for help, Mrs. Rose Casey, a close friend of the family. During her frequent visits to the home, she had taken an interest in Ruby, often offering advice and insight into life. She has become more of a maternal figure than a stranger. Ruby will go to her for help; the pregnancy can no longer be hidden. Under intense scrutiny and a barrage of questions from Mrs. Bogle, as to the identity of the father, Ruby reveals that her husband, Mr. Bogle is the father. Mrs. Bogle's wrath comes down upon both their heads. Mr. Bogle tries denying having anything to do with her pregnancy, but Ruby is incessant in her insistence that he is responsible for her condition, even telling Mrs. Bogle that it happened each time he stayed home from work. He recants his story, turning the blame on her.

She is a little whore. What was I supposed to do when she kept coming on to me?" Moreover, you know that I am a man and we are weak. You had no right to bring a young girl into the house and leave her here alone with me. When was the last time we had sex? You claim to be going through menopause, experiencing dryness and hot flashes. I have needs."

Mrs. Bogle choosing to forgive her husband, orders Ruby out of her house. With no place to go Ruby packs her bags, drags them out the door, down the street for a half mile, wearily ending up on

# The Odyssey of Survival

Mrs. Casey's doorsteps. The friends disagree over the treatment to be exacted to Ruby. Mrs. Bogle wishes her dead, but Mrs. Casey putting their friendship in danger, points out the facts. "It's your husband who is the perpetrator of the crime. He is a married fifty-one year old pervert, who cajoled an innocent sixteen year old into having relations with him. She was a victim of her own circumstances, who needs *help*, not banishment."

But Mrs. Bogle is adamant; Ruby is no longer welcome in her home. Against the wishes of Mrs. Bogle, Mrs. Casey takes in young Ruby. In her heart Mrs. Bogle, knows the truth, but she sides with her husband. She loves him and is committed to their marriage. She lays down the law for Ruby. The child will not bear his name, nor will her husband have anything to do with Ruby or her child. And you Rose, if you choose to associate yourself with her and take her into your home, you can count this the end of our friendship. I never want to see either one of you again." With those last words Mrs. Bogle slams the door after ushering her best friend and Ruby out. Ruby moves into the Casey's home, where she lives until she delivers her baby. Mr. Bogle makes no attempt to contact her. He has conveniently forgotten that a young girl, whom he had taken advantage of, was carrying his child. On November 3, 1924, unknown to her mother, Ruby Grant gives birth to a baby girl who she named Vira Miranda Grant. Except for the kindness of a stranger, Ruby and her child are alone in the world.

Six months after the birth of her baby Ruby finds work in another household. This time she wears a permanent scowl on her face, defusing the intentions of any man from looking twice in her direction. Mrs. Casey becomes the godmother of her baby girl, loving the infant like her own. Life is good for Ruby and Vira. Mrs. Casey provides a stable environment in which young Vira thrives, developing a love for the books read to her nightly.

The backwoods of St. Elizabeth is the farthest thing from her mind, until three years later when the mailman delivers a telegram from home. Holding the brown envelope in her shaking hand, Ruby wonders what could be so important for her mother to communicate with her with such urgency. Fearfully she looks at her friend. "Go ahead, open the telegram, it must be important." Tearing open the envelope she stops breathing as she reads the message.

"Come home now. Mama Sick. Near death."

Stunned Ruby hands the piece of paper to Mrs. Casey. "What am I going to do?" she asks. Mrs. Casey puts her arms around Ruby, drawing her close.

"Well, there is not much you can do. This says your mother is on her death bed, you have to return home to see her and help your younger sisters cope with her illness."

"But how am I going to show up with Vira? They don't even know that I have a child."

"You are not thinking of taking this child to St. Elizabeth now. Are you?"

What else can I do? Who am I going to leave her with? Moreover, I don't know how long I'll be gone."

"Ruby, listen to me, your mother is ill and your family needs you. Get your stuff together and I'll take you to the bus stop in the morning. Vira will be fine with me. Don't you trust me to take care of her? Remember she is my goddaughter and I love her."

"I know you love her, but we have never been apart before, I'm afraid she'll miss me too much and won't know me when I come back."

"I understand your concern, but don't worry my dear. I promise to take good care of her and she'll know who you are regardless of how long you're gone."

## The Odyssey of Survival

Kneeling to Vira's level, Ruby takes her daughter's hand in hers, wiping tears from her eyes she speak softly to her.

"Sweetheart mama has to go away for awhile. My mother is sick and I need to go be with her. Aunty Rose is going to take care of you while I am gone. I want you to be good for her, listen to her and be a good girl for Mama. Ok?"

"Mama, where are you going?"

"I have to go see my mother in St. Elizabeth."

"Where is St. Elizabeth?"

"It's where I was born. My mother still lives there and she is sick so I have to go see her. I love you and will be back as soon as I can."

"Ok Mama."

For six years tragic events prevent Ruby from returning to her daughter. Soon after arriving at her mother's bedside, Ruby's mother succumbed to her illness, dying in the presence of her children. Ruby has no choice, but to remain home to care for her two younger sisters. Her father had died from pneumonia years earlier. As the eldest child she is now head of the household. Ruby resents her siblings, and hates the primitive lifestyle even more. She misses Vira terribly, but she finds comfort in the knowledge that she is being cared for by her godmother. In St. Elizabeth Ruby tries adjusting to the way of life. She had forgotten how hard life was and is constantly being criticized by the neighbors for spilling the water she carries on her head from the river. Her sisters resented her for her airs and manners she learned in Kingston and tells her she thinks she is better than they are because she lived in town. Silently she moves around the small hut, brushing tears from her eyes before they can be witnessed and laughed at. The country is no place for the pretty girl who has grown accustomed to city living.

# The Odyssey of Survival

In Kingston she was guaranteed an education, and had begun making plans to attend school when that cursed telegram arrived. She had access to modern facilities, and above all, was loved by her friend and daughter. Ruby longs for her baby, but cannot breathe a word about her existence to her sisters. It was best for Vira to remain in Kingston. Ruby assumes the responsibilities of the home doing backbreaking work in the field to feed the family. She endures the separation from her child, communicating by snail pace mail with her friend. Ruby knows that Vira has grown into a bright little girl, and is doing well in school, but she missed her daughter's laughter and chatter. When will she hold her in her arms again?"

Vira has stopped missing her mother. In the past six years she has almost forgotten about her; vague memories of another person drifts in and out of her mind when her name is mentioned, but she has everything a little girl wants and is happy.

During the fifth year in St. Elizabeth, Ruby meets and shortly after marries Charles Grant. Months later Ruby confesses the existence of her daughter to her husband. Charles is livid at her seemingly deception and refuses to listen to her reasoning. They already have her two sisters living with them; he has no intentions of allowing another family member into their home. After many arguments, Ruby defiantly decides that regardless of what happens or what others think of her, she wants her daughter with her. The lying must end. She discloses to her sisters that she has a child and they have a niece. With that out of the way Ruby travels to Kingston to bring Vira home.

Vira has been happy with her godmother, but her happiness doesn't last long. Destiny catches up with her. Six years after being left in the care of her godmother whom she now calls Mama, her world is shattered. One morning a vaguely familiar woman shows up. She holds young Vira tightly in her arms telling her how happy she is to see her.

# The Odyssey of Survival

Twisting out of her arms Vira goes to her godmother's side. "Who is that Mama?" she asks.

"Baby come here. Don't you remember me? I am your mother."

She looks up at the mother she knows for answers.

"Baby this is your mother. Don't you remember her? Remember I told you about her and that she was coming to see you."

"I remember her just a little bit, but you are my mother now."

"No baby. I love you, but Ruby is your mother and she loves you. She had to go away but now she is back. Go give her a hug."

Reluctantly, Vira walks to her mother, allowing Ruby to hug her stiff body. With fire in her eyes Ruby looks at Mrs. Casey.

"You stole my daughter. She doesn't even know who I am anymore. I trusted you to care for her for me, but only God knows what you have been telling her about me, she won't even come to me."

"I did nothing of the sort. When you leave a three-year-old child for six years, after a while they forget. Those are the formative years. That's where their memory begins to form. They know who cares for them, who comes when they cry at night and who feeds them. I constantly tell her about you, so it's not my fault if she doesn't remember you."

"Well I am here to take her back with me, so she'll remember who I am soon enough."

"What? You didn't tell me you were coming to get her. In your letter you said you were coming to see her. She is doing well in school, and in piano. Why would you want to take her away from all of this, back to that woodland? What type of life is she going to have there?"

"She will be just fine."

"Ruby listen to me. You remember how much you hated St. Elizabeth? You were always talking about how awful life is there. Why would you want to deprive your own child of an opportunity to have a good life here with me and take her back to the country?"

"It hasn't killed anyone yet, and it won't kill her either. I'll be leaving in the morning taking her with me. I appreciate all you have done for her, but I need her at home. I'm now married to a fine man. My two sisters are living with us. She will have many people to care for her. She'll be fine."

Mrs. Casey tries reasoning with Ruby, but nothing she says has any effect on her. She has come to fetch her daughter and nothing is going to dissuade her.

"Ruby, leave the child with me. She is no trouble. I love having her. Look at her school report. She is doing very well. Leave her alone. Why do you want to disrupt her life? Leaving her here with me guarantees her a future, she will be educated, have opportunities to help herself and ultimately help you. What is there for her in St. Elizabeth?"

"I am thankful to you for taking care of her for me. You did a great job. She looks good, speaks well, and has grown so big. But she is *my* child and I need her. I'm about to have another baby, and need her to help me in the house and in the field with the animals."

Horrified at the thought of her precious godchild working in the field? Mrs. Casey begged for reconsideration.

"You need her to work in the field? Are you crazy? How can you even think about putting this child to work milking, moving and caring for animals?
That's no life for her. How can you be so cruel to do that to this precious little girl?"

# The Odyssey of Survival

"She must come home with me; I'm now married and can take care of her. Everyone survives, she will be fine. You have grown her up to be too soft, and she needs some toughening up."

This is the end of the discussion, nothing Rose Casey says can change Ruby's mind, she has come to collect her child and there was no dissuading her. The following morning, Vira is pried from the arms of her godmother and slapped by her mother to stop crying. Vira is dragged by the hand out the door, down the street, onto the waiting bus. Twenty-four hours later the bus reaches its destination. Vira is unceremoniously thrust into a new family. She cries for days, but soon learns that in this new household, in which she is an unwelcomed intrusion, there is no place for emotions. No one cares about your feelings. Chores have to be done. There is no tolerance for anything else. At nine years old she has her share of work to do. The darkness and smelly animals around the house frightens her. No one cares.

Life in Kingston had been good. The homes have kitchens where water comes out of faucets, toilets are located inside with indoor plumbing, food is purchased at the markets, not farmed and reaped and meat comes from the butcher shop, not killed and dragged into the kitchen where it is pickled and hung from the ceiling until the last portion is hacked off and eaten. Light comes out of bulbs by the flick of a switch and there are tiles, carpet or rugs on the floor. Vira is astonished to see dirt flooring and on alternate days her aunts sprinkle water on the dirt to keep the dust from flying around, then it's swept clean. Vira is petrified to go into the disgusting place called the latrine. In that small filthy room, rats, roaches, scorpions and lizards lurk in the dark corners waiting to feed. She finds sitting over the dark hole disgusting because there is no telling what will crawl up her leg.

How she longs for her bed with its soft mattress and warm sheets! Here the bedding is a rough flour bag filled with some type of smelly stuff that pokes into her body, and crackles with each move.

"I'll never forgive my mother for disrupting my life, bringing me to this horrible place." She laments.

"I hate her."

Vira's life has changed. Now she has to work in the fields, care for the animals, milk the cows, gather the eggs and prepare breakfast before attending school in the mornings. On her daily trek to school she daydreams of getting away from this awful place, those two mean aunts who make fun of her each time she opens her mouth, that loud man who she refuses to call daddy, and this woman. If only she could run away. But where would she go? There is no place to run. She has not heard from her beloved Mama. Maybe she doesn't love me after all, she muses. That's what Ruby says. Maybe she is right. She likes her life at home as living in an open cage with a pregnant, hungry lioness. Seven long miserable years pass. She has been condemned with no possibility of release. Except, Oh God, if only a young man would come along on a horse or foot or even in a wheelchair. It doesn't matter how he gets here. A man asking for her hand in marriage is her only escape. At sixteen she is sullen. Her spirit has been broken. She seeks out the darkest corners in which to retreat, hoping to avoid detection while finding a few moments of peace from the hateful members of the household. Unwontedly, Vira has attracted the attention of Billy Starcky while sitting in her corner. Something about Vira strikes a cord of compassion and emotional unrest in the young man. Even though, on his last visit, he had been shown the door, and told not to come back when he tried telling Ruby about the God who created the world and loves her. He decides to face the wrath of Miss Ruby and return one more time, just to catch a glimpse of the sad eyed young girl. Miss Ruby is furious when she opens her door and sees him standing there.

"Didn't I tell you not to come back to my house? I don't want to hear anything more about your God." All five feet of her challenge the tall young man.

# The Odyssey of Survival

"Where is your daughter?" he asked, "Maybe she would like to hear about God."

Her frame shakes with indignation. Her voice is almost a snarl. "My daughter's whereabouts is none of your business; get away from my door boy."

"I am not a boy madam, and I will leave as soon as I speak with your daughter or you tell me where I can find her."

"You are insolent too, have you been seeing my daughter behind my back. If I find out you two have been sneaking around I'll kill her."

"No madam. We have not been fooling around, as a matter of fact I have never spoken to her but now I would like to, if you don't mind."

"I do mind, now get out of here."

"With all due respect madam, I am going nowhere until I speak with your daughter."

"People these days have no respect, if the only way to get rid of you is to tell you where she is then, go. She is in the field moving the animals."

"What" he exclaimed, "You have your daughter out moving animals? That is no work for a young lady"

Miss Ruby replied, "What business is it of yours? Get out of my house, and never let me see your ugly face here again."

The door closes in his face. He leaves the house, but now he has a reason to return to the home. He has to save this girl.

# The Odyssey of Survival

Unaware of what had transpired at home between her mother and the man she has not met, Vira arrives home exhausted and hungry, only to be met with a barrage of abuse. The unthinkable has happened. A man has shown interest in her daughter and it certainly cannot be allowed to continue. Miss Ruby contemplates. Has Vira found a way to encourage this man? Had she somehow slipped from under the watchful eyes of Miss Ruby and committed the sin of speaking to a member of the opposite sex? This has to be stopped now.

Billy however, is not fazed by Miss Ruby's wrath. He decides in his heart that he loves this girl to whom he has never even spoken. He has not been able to get her out of his mind. Instead of going crazy with his imagination running wild, he decides to pay her a visit. For the second time he commits a carnal sin by showing up on Miss Ruby's doorstep. This time he doesn't only inquire about her daughter. He asks for her hand in marriage.

Miss Ruby shakes with fury. WHAT! An illiterate farmer is asking for her daughter's hand in marriage? This is absurd. What has befallen her? What sins has this girl committed, to bring such a disgrace upon the family?

"Get away from my door. "You will never marry any daughter of mine."

The door slams in his face. Vira is standing in the corner listening to the exchange. Her angel of deliverance for whom she has been praying every night has come, but her mother is chasing him away. Tears swell up in Vira's eyes. She is forever doomed to live in this horrible state. But love is a strange compelling thing. Not even Miss Ruby's indignant treatment can daunt Billy's pursuit of Vira. Relentlessly he pursues her, showing up at the door regardless of Miss Ruby's threats and verbal abuse. He wants Vira and refuses to give up asking for her to be his wife. Six weeks later, Miss Ruby relents. She has gotten tired of his constant badgering. Throwing her hands up in the air she shouts.

# The Odyssey of Survival

"Oh what the hell, marry her, she is not much use in the fields anyway, still too soft and spoiled from living in Kingston. Go ahead; take her off my hands one less mouth to feed."

They can get married but Miss Ruby inserts a contingency to her approval. Their firstborn will have to be given to her. This request is preposterous but to achieve his goals, Billy agrees to the deal. There is no courtship. No long walks to learn about each other, no gazing longingly into each others eyes nor any engagement party, no choosing of dresses or flowers or bridal party, or planning the menu. No whispering into each other's ears. There is no contact between them. Vira's mother tells her that she will be getting married to Billy Starcky on a prearranged date. She so desperately wants to escape her mother's clutches that marriage to anyone will be good. She has seen him from afar on a few occasions and admires his tall, dark handsomeness. Becoming his wife sounds good to her. Secretly her heart rejoices, but she reveals no outward expression of delight. The prospect of getting away from Mother is exhilarating.
She would have married an eighty-year-old man with one leg and one eye. Miss Ruby dominates the wedding plans. On one occasion Vira tries making a suggestion about her own wedding plans. She is rebuffed and punished.

"Sit down and be quiet. You are still a child to be seen and not heard."
Vira ventures to speak again.

"Do you think you are a woman in here? Let me show you who the woman in this house is."

Vira flees from the house running into the field with her Mother in hot pursuit threatening to whip her senseless to teach her a lesson in respect and obedience. To escape the beating Vira climbs a tree. Disobeying her Mother's orders to get down so she could get what is coming to her. Miss Ruby, not to be outdone chops down the tree to get her hands on her. Vira receives her last whipping.

# The Odyssey of Survival

Wedding day is here, and even in the worst situation something humorous presents itself. The bride is beautiful and the groom dashing as he proudly stands by his bride. Everything is going smoothly until the reception, which of course will be held at Miss Ruby's. The bride laughs out loud to a compliment paid to her. Miss Ruby's head spins around as the sound of the laughter hits her ears.

Recognizing the laugh as Vira's, Ruby hastens over to her; with a scowl on her face.

"What was that? Do you think you are a woman now because there is a ring on your finger? Get inside and stay there. You are not going anywhere tonight."

This brings a sudden end to the festivities as Ruby clears everyone from her home. The wedding reception is over, and she intends to apply a whipping to Vira. Billy is furious. No way is he going to allow this woman to beat his wife and he certainly is not going home without her. He had waited months for this day. He will take his bride home to his bed. It takes all of his persuasive talents to convince Miss Ruby to release his wife. After several hours of talking; Miss Ruby listens to reason and the relieved couple leave to start their new life. Miss Ruby's intentions are to control even the consummation of the marriage. She lost this battle, but not the war. It simply gets added to the list of resentments and the mutual hate between mother and daughter. Within the first three months of the marriage, Vira is pregnant. The baby is stillborn. The next three pregnancies all end the same way, each child dying at birth or soon after birth. Two years later the fifth baby is born. It's a girl, and she survives infancy. Her name is Amelia Grace. After much praying and sleepless nights during her first three months, her parents exhale. They watch over her with eagle's eyes, afraid she might also be taken away from them. During the first nine months of her life, grandma shows up to collect her bounty. She had exacted a promise from them to give their first child to her in exchange for their freedom to marry. Billy and Vira fiercely defend themselves against Miss Ruby. They refuse to give her up and the wrath of hell is loosened. To protect their precious

# The Odyssey of Survival

baby from being stolen, the family decides to move, in an attempt, to get away from Miss Ruby. Amelia delights her father as she grows into a toddler, learning to walk and talk, pulling his beard to get his attention.

Billy is a successful farmer in St. Elizabeth, where he owns land and livestock, his decision to leave his hometown to protect his new family has serious consequences. His land and possessions will be left behind. For their protection he leaves it all behind, moving his family to Mount Felix, St. Thomas. He's now an employee, working the fields of others to support his family. Eventually, by hard work and saving what he could he buys a few acres of land, but Billy is unable to achieve the success he'd left behind. He has a brother already living in St. Thomas, and together they try to make good for their families.

In rapid succession more children are born into the household. In ten years they have five children- three girls and two boys. Amelia, the eldest cares for the younger ones, attending school only when possible, depending on whether their mother was having another baby or if the baby was ill. The older ones have to remain at home to care for the younger ones, allowing their mother time to care for the newborn. There is a string of children, one in the womb, another on the hip, a little one crawling around on the floor, and one hanging on to the hem of a skirt. The countryside is harsh and provides a challenge to the poor. Life is hard, and survival depends quite a bit on the cooperation of neighbors and friends. Bartering is a way of life, trading one produce for another or ground produce for meat. Even harsher than the countryside is the treatment meted out to the family by their mother. She is a strict disciplinarian, abusive and cruel. Her own mother had shown her no love and she does not know how to express love to her children. The only love she had known, that of her godmother has been forgotten, and resentment has hardened her heart. Sadly enough, even the love of her husband is unable to penetrate the hard core which had built up over the years. Vira had not learned the art of loving, only the cycle of abuse and neglect. She now lives what she learned. Husband and children suffer at her hands.

# The Odyssey of Survival

After a heated disagreement, Vira chases her husband out of the house with a machete, threatening to chop him to pieces. Seizing a machete she bolts after Billy.

"I'm going to chop you up!" she shrieks. Billy darts from behind one tree to the next, trying to conceal himself from her.

"You miserable man, this is your last night on earth."

Billy's agility keeps him out of her range. Exhausted, she returns home. Trudging into the house she pushes the children out of her way, as she heads for the bedroom. Furiously she yanks shirts, pants, and underwear, and shoes out of the closet. She can scarcely see over the heap of clothes as she marches determinedly outside the house. Dumping her burden unceremoniously on the ground, she returns to the kitchen, returning with the oil pan. Vira pours kerosene oil over the pile, strikes a match, flinging it on top of the pile of clothing.

The children watch in horror from the safety of the house as every piece of their father's clothing is burned to ash. Smelling smoke, Billy cautiously approaches the house, only to see a smoldering pile in the front yard. She notices him and venom spews from her mouth. With the kerosene pan at her feet and the box of matches in her hand, she threatens to douse him adding his ash to that of his clothing.

"What am I to do woman?"

"To hell with you man. You better sleep outside this house tonight or I'll kill you. I will pour hot oil down your ears while you are asleep."

Billy spends the night in a mango tree. Vira spends the night under the tree.

"You better stay up there because if you come down I'm going to kill you."

# The Odyssey of Survival

Billy stayed. Sleep begins making his eyes heavy. It takes superhuman strength to remain in the boughs of his tree. He falls asleep, and falls out of the tree. He bounces, thwacks and thuds until he hits the ground hard, sustaining serious injuries. His screams awaken Vira, who gets up from her place, looks at him, and uses her foot to poke him in the side testing for life. He groans.

"Get up off the ground and get inside the house. You made me sleep under this tree all night like an animal. I should kill you for that."

Together they limp into the house, where children are asleep all over the floor. Billy is a loving and kind man but he lacks the ability to teach Vira how to love and trust. She treats the children like animals. She has no regard for their lives and it's only the mercy of God that keeps them alive.

"Come here pickney I'm going to kill you."

Whimpering like a wounded puppy Amelia slips away from the left hand which smashed into her face.

"How many times do I have to tell you not to play with those lice-infested, hungry-belly, black pickneys from down the lane?"

"Sorry, mama, they were playing dandy-shandy and it looked like fun."

Approaching Amelia's hiding place Vira lifts the whip above her head.

"Looked like fun, there are enough of you in this house to make your own fun – come here."

Blows rain down on Amelia, held fast in one hand. Squirming, ducking, twisting, scurrying around, she tries dodging the punishment. Deflated the screaming child falls down, but the beating has no end. Kicks to her stomach bring howls of pain.

"Woman what are you doing to the child? Stop kicking her, give that to me, have you gone crazy?"

"Come over here and I'll give you your share. You stand outside and let her to play with those dirty pickneys from down the lane after I told them not to."

"Vira have you gone mad. Is that a reason to beat the child like this?"

She turns her fury on Billy. Loosening her grip on Amelia, who crawls away. Vira gives Billy his share of verbal beating adding a few licks with the belt.

With each pregnancy, Billy wishes for a son. The second and third children are girls, named Victoria and Lynnette; he does not give up hope. A son will show up soon. The fourth birth fulfills his dream; to his delight he has a son. His joy quickly turns to disappointment when Vira refuses to make his son his namesake. Instead she names him Lester. His father dearly loves him but for reasons known only to her, his mother hates him. He meets hell at her hands. She deals with him very harshly; nothing he does is right in her sight.

On more than one occasion, water had to be thrown on him to revive him after a beating. One shadowy night, Vira decides that Lester needs to be punished more than normal for a minor infraction. Eight-year-old Lester is afraid of the dark.

"Lester where are you boy? Why do I have to call you more than once?"

Lester is nowhere to be found.

"Where is that boy? Amelia, Victoria where is your brother?"

"I don't know where he is mama. He jumped off the bed and went outside."

# The Odyssey of Survival

"Lester, boy I'm going to take the skin off your black ass. Where are you? You had better be in the house before my spit dry. I'm not going to call you again."

"Here I am mama."

"Where have you been boy? Why do I have to call you more than one time? Come here I am going to teach you a lesson you'll never forget."

"Mama, mama, I was only playing with John down the lane. Please don't beat me. I'll never do it again. I promise."

Grabbing Lester by the arm Vira drags him to a tree.

"Didn't I tell you not to leave the house?" A fist slams into his tiny face.

"I'm tired of looking for you. You need to learn to do what I tell you to do. Once and for all I'm going to teach you a lesson. Since you want to be outside, you are going to stay outside."

Horrified Lester scrambles to get away. He twists around behind his mother trying to loosen her grip on him. Dragging Lester to the back of the house Vira gets a piece of rope all the time with Lester bawling behind her. The girls look on in horror as mother ties their brother to a tree.

"You want to be outside, now you will be outside."

Vira walks away from her son, closing her ears to his howling. Billy comes home to chaos. He begs Vira to loosen the boy. He attempts to set him free, but is halted in his steps when his wife flings a stone after him hitting him in the back of his head.

# The Odyssey of Survival

"If you touch him tonight believe me you are a dead man."

"How long are you going to leave the child tied to a tree like an animal? Don't you think he has learned his lesson by now?"

"He is going to spend the night out there. I'm tired of talking to him, he needs to be taught a lesson to obey me the first time I talk to him and come the first time I call him."

"Are you crazy? What has gone wrong with you? You cannot leave the child outside tied to a tree all night. It's dark and dangerous. An animal walking through the yard during the night could kill him. Let him go, beat him if you have to; but please release him and bring him inside."

"He stays where he is. If he gets eaten alive; good riddance. One less mouth to feed. I'm tired of all of them anyway, and if you keep pestering me about it, you'll join him out there."

Lester bellows and bawls. He screams begging mama to let him go into the house. It's all to no avail. Mama turns a deaf ear to him leaving him tied to a tree in the dark yard all night. His siblings cling to one another, helplessly crying for him. His father begs for his release, but Vira tells him to "shut up," or he too will be put out of the house. Somehow Lester survives the night and is cut loose, exhausted and broken the following morning. Lester cannot escape her wrath. The roof of the house becomes his bedroom another night when he fled there to escape a beating. He screams and begs, but mother is unmoved. No amount of pleading changes Vira's mind to let him in the house. He doesn't escape the beating either. Lester suffers greatly. Vira hears of a stranger needing someone to work the fields and care for his animals. She gives Lester away to the farmer. If she never sees him again it would not be a day too soon. She doesn't care if she never sees him again, and cares even less about his education. At the end of his usefulness to the stranger Lester is returned to the family.

# The Odyssey of Survival

His welcome: his mother lifts her foot high, kicking him down the steps into the front yard, where she steps over his limp body leaving his siblings to come to his rescue.

Another son is born. He is named Leroy. He is treated no better than Lester. He also endures murderous beatings. One hot day Leroy is on his way home from school, he sees a truck approaching in the distance and decides to jump onto the back as it passes by. His grip loosens and he tumbles off the truck. He is thrown under the back wheel, which runs over him. Eye witness runs to his side; doing what they can to help him. He is alive. They pick him up placing him in the back of a pickup truck, taking him home to his mother. After hearing what caused the accident, Vira gives Leroy a beating, which came closer to killing him than the accident did. He receives no medical treatment for his head injuries. Leroy has never been the same again. He has recovered from his external injuries, but his internal and head injuries needed medical attention. He now has trouble learning to read and write and remembering his timetables is out of the question. Leroy is classified as a simple boy, but mama doesn't care.

"The Lord is my light and my salvation, whom shall I fear. The Lord is the strength of my life of whom shall I be afraid. When the wicked come upon me to eat up my flesh, they stumble and fall…wait on the Lord, be of good courage and he shall strength thy heart. Wait I say, on the Lord." Psalms 37: 1-2 &14 (KJV)

***Life question:*** *Spousal abuse is intolerable, but child abuse and neglect tug at the heart of everyone. (Almost everyone). If a parent has a tendency to abuse their spouse, do you think that's a red light to child abuse? And how is it stopped? How can an abused child avoid becoming an abusive adult?*

**Answer:**

## *Chapter Two*

## LOSS

Mother is gone to the market leaving eleven year old Amelia home to care for her four younger siblings. Billy has traveled to another parish, Clarendon to work. The mailman delivers a telegram. Amelia, because of her frequent absence from school is unable to read the telegram, but her instincts tell her that it's important.

Looking at the folded message in her hands Amelia wonders what to do. Her curiosity has gotten the better of her. She runs next door to Mrs. Reeve.

"Good morning, Mrs. Reeve. This telegram just came for mama but she went to the market. I think it is important, can you please read it and tell me what it says?"

"Where's your mother? She knows how to read."

She walks around here with her nose in the air pretending to be better than the rest of us.

"Where is she?"

Impatiently shifting her weight from one foot to the other Amelia anxiously replies.

"She went to the market and daddy went to Clarendon to work. Can you please tell me what it says?"

Grudgingly Mrs. Reeve opens the telegram. As she reads her eyes grow wide. Looking up over her glasses at the child she says. "Your father is sick unto death; your mother needs to go to Clarendon now. Handing the telegram back to Amelia she continues.

"By the way tell your mother she owes me one shilling for reading this."

Amelia walks home with tears streaming down her face. Impatiently she waits for her mother to return, she goes to the door often trying to get a glimpse of her as she comes down the lane. She sees her. Jumping off the last step; Amelia dashes down the dirt path to meet her mother.

"What are you doing out here didn't I tell you to stay inside with the other children until I come back?"

"Mama, mama, something bad happened to daddy, you have to go to Clarendon now."

"What are you talking about? Nothing happened to your father. What is that you have in your hand?"

"It's a telegram."

"I know what it is, give it to me."

"I know you're going to beat me but I know something is wrong so I asked Mrs. Reeve to tell me what it says. She said daddy is sick and you have to go to him now. What's wrong with him mama is he going to die?"

"I don't know child. Here carry these. I'm tired."

Vira opens the telegram and sits down heavily on the side of the road. She begins crying.

# The Odyssey of Survival

"Oh my God. What am I going to do?"

"Amelia your father is sick; I have to go to him. I need you to be a good girl and take care of your sisters and brother for me. Can you do that?"

"Yes mama, I can take care of them. Are you going to bring daddy back home with you?"

"Yes baby I will bring daddy back home with me. Now go inside, I have to find someone to take me to Clarendon tonight."

Vira's heart plunges to her feet, she wants to sit down and cry, but has no time for that. Hastily she makes her way to the neighbor trying to find transportation for her journey. The telegram had been sent two days earlier. What is his condition now?

"Mr. Moses, my husband is sick, I need to go to Clarendon where he is in the hospital can you give me a ride?"

"Sorry to hear about your husband, but I can't leave here now. Maybe Mr. Jimmy can take you."

Running to Mr. Jimmy she screams.

"Mr. Jimmy I must get to Clarendon tonight. Can you give me a ride?"

"Mrs. Starkey, I am sorry to hear that. Mr. Billy is a good man so I'll take you but not before in the morning, it's almost dark now and it's a day's journey."

"I know its almost dark Mr. Jimmy but I have to go tonight. He has been sick for two days and the message sounds serious can we please go tonight."

"It's dark and dangerous out there and I am tired. Go home and get some rest, we'll leave at daybreak."

# The Odyssey of Survival

"Thank you Mr. Jimmy. God bless you."

Vira rushes down the long hospital corridor to the nurses' station, waving the telegram above her head, announcing her name, and demanding to see her husband. Calmly a nurse steps in front of her; she places her arms around Vira's shoulders leading her away to a room.

"Where's my husband? I got this telegram and came as soon as I could. Which room is he in?"

"Mrs. Starcky, I wish there was another way to tell you this but your husband passed away yesterday. We did everything we could. He was admitted with severe abdominal pain and throwing up blood. His appendix had ruptured. We tried to save him, we did all we could, but he didn't make it. I'm sorry."

"No, don't tell me foolishness, where is my Billy? I want to see my husband now. Get me the doctor or somebody in charge. He can't be dead. You must be talking about the wrong person. I want to see him now. I want to see Billy now."

"I'll get a doctor."

Falling to her knees onto the floor she curls herself up into a ball, lifting her face upwards, wailing.

"Oh God don't let my Billy be dead. Please don't take him away from me; he's all I have. Billy, Billy Oh God help me."

She Crumbles face down, the nurse holds her by the shoulders trying desperately to lift her to her feet. It takes two orderlies to get her seated.

"Leave me alone if Billy is dead I want to die too. I can't live without him. Billy, where are you? Come nurse show me his room you must have made a mistake I'm talking about Billy Starcky the tall dark man who came from Mt Felix just a few days ago to work.

## The Odyssey of Survival

He wouldn't die and leave me. Let me see him, show him to me. Maybe he's just in a coma, when he hears my voice he'll come around. Billy, where are you?"

Mrs. Starcky, we understand your distress and sympathize with your loss but you must listen to us. Your husband passed away. He is dead."

She raises her downcast head above her shoulders and backwards, opens her mouth screaming like a demented person.

"Billy don't leave me, O Billy I love you."

Vira goes into meltdown. She is sedated and admitted into the hospital. Awakening the following morning reality sets in. Her husband was dead she was lying in the same hospital in which he had died. What is she going to do? What is she going to do with the remains of her beloved husband? With no money to transport his body home Vira has to make the unpleasant decision of leaving the body behind, signing it over to the hospital for their disposal in whatever manner they choose. One week later Vira drags herself home. Five pairs of sad eyes look at her.

"Where is Daddy?" they ask. "Where have you been? We are hungry."

Breaking the news to the children is the worst thing she has ever done. Daddy is dead; they will never see him again. How on earth was she going to provide for herself and these five children? But that has to wait. The reality of his death has just begun sinking in, and the enormity of it causes her to experience a break with reality. She becomes hysterical, screaming, howling and wallowed in her grief. The neighbors rush out of their homes to see what had happened. The news of Billy's death spreads and everyone comes by expressing sympathy and offering whatever help they can. Vira, unable to function is huddled into a tight ball in her lonely bed. Eleven-year-old Amelia has no time to grieve for her father; she is left with the responsibility of caring for herself and her siblings.

## The Odyssey of Survival

They have nothing to eat except the scraps neighbors choose to pass their way.

Two weeks later a disheveled and confused Vira ventures out of her bedroom. Her eyes are swollen almost shut and she has lost weight. With her husband's death, there is no family to come to her aid. Her sisters have become estranged from her, and communication with her mother has long ceased. Billy has family in the vicinity but no one comes to help, because Vira had kept her husband away from his family. They had not been welcome into their home. During a disagreement between Vira and Billy, he visited his brother, Errol's home in an attempt to calm down. Retrieving his hat from the back of the chair, placing it firmly on his head while making long angry strides towards the door, he is confronted. Vira, hands akimbo demands an answer.

"Where do you think you're going?"

"I'm going over to Errol's house."

"If you think you're leaving me here alone with these children so you can go idle with that no good brother of yours, you're making a sad mistake."

Reaching for the doorknob Billy takes another step forward.
With feet planted apart and blazing eyes Vira commanded him to get away from the door, or else.

"Or else what?' He asked, not waiting for a reply he leaves the house slamming the door behind him.

Within a few minutes of Billy entering Errol's home the sudden noise of shattered glass and thuds against the walls startles them. Running outside to investigate they find Vira pelting the house with rocks, threatening to break every window, then kick in the door until her husband leaves.

# The Odyssey of Survival

"Go home to your crazy wife. I love you my brother, but as long as you have that maniac woman as your wife I'll have nothing to do with you. I will not visit your home, and please don't come back here, because if she ever lifts her hand to stone my house or harm anything of mine again, I swear I'll chop her to pieces."

That is the last encounter between the two families. Errol hears of his brother's death and instantly blames Vira. Helping her with his nieces and nephews is out of the question. He has never forgiven her for stoning his home and wants nothing to do with her. To make matters worst Billy's body had been left at the hospital to the mercy of the authorities. His family is furious with Vira; they blame her for his having gone to Clarendon in the first place, believing that he had gone just to get away from her. Now he is dead and there is not even his body to be buried, no funeral to attend, and no graveside to leave flowers, no head stone on which to carve the family's name. They hate her. All the land owned by Billy now belongs to his brother Errol, who takes over the working of the land keeping all the produce and animals for him, never casting an eye in the bereaved family's direction. The children are hungry to the point of malnutrition, but he ignores them. Vira is a wreck. She cries day and night, devoid of any idea that her children need to be cared for.

Sitting on the bank of the river, the dirty laundry forgotten, Vira watches the birds idly swooping up and down catching small fishes. The soft whisper of the wind in the trees and the splashing of the water on the rocks create a serene cocoon. Vira is anything but calm. The turmoil within her has reached fever pitch. Then an idea forms within her mind. As if being led by an unseen hand; Vira walks away from her laundry. She wades deep into the murky water. Taking a deep breath she plunges herself face down. Unable to swim she sinks like a rock, as her lungs fill with water. Coming to wash her cloths a neighbor catches a glimpse of a body sinking in the river. Yelling for help she jumps in, help comes running, and they drag Vira's almost lifeless body from the water. A retired nurse performs CPR. A crowd gathers as she splutters back to consciousness. A police officer delivers her home to her frightened children. The young children are pitiful. They have no idea how to survive. Amelia begs the neighbors for food, receiving scraps and whatever else they can spare. When Vira recovers she is hungry. She sends Amelia and Victoria to the field to find Mr. Grounds who had promised to help. Mr. Grounds sees an opportunity, and grabs it with both hands. He will supply the family with provision from his field, but there will be a price attached. He has the food and she has young daughters. The following morning the girls accompany Mr. Grounds into his field to collect food. He fills their baskets with yam, banana, potatoes, breadfruit, peas and beans. His roaming hands find themselves under their dresses and between their legs as often as he can. He tries forcing his sexual organ onto Amelia. She pushes him away, jumps up and they run as fast as they can, while carrying baskets of food on their heads. Amelia and Victoria escape the first attack but they know it will be short lived. They cannot tell mama what had happened to them, nor can they refuse to get the supplies so badly needed by the household. Putting their heads together they devise a plan to escape Mr. Ground's advances.

Sharpening one of mother's knives on a stone; hiding it under their clothing, they prepare for their next encounter with Mr. Grounds. Pain will be inflicted the next time hands begin roaming in private places. Back in the field the baskets are again filled with food, and Mr. Grounds begin groping in private places. Forgetting their brilliant plan, they flee. Trying to escape Amelia's foot becomes tangled in roots tossing her to the ground where a piece of branch embeds itself into her ankle. Ignoring the pain in her foot she jumps up and climbs a mango tree. In her haste, she loses her balance, falling out of the tree headfirst landing on her back. Victoria, hearing the thud and scream flies from her hiding place to her sister's side. She finds Amelia lying on the ground. Victoria grabs her head up in her hands pleading.

"Amelia you dead? Get up girl him coming. You dead Amelia?"

# The Odyssey of Survival

Dazed and unable to answer Amelia lies prostrate on the ground with Victoria by her side begging her to speak to her. About two hours later Amelia tentatively gets to her feet. They scramble home carrying what food Victoria can carry on her head. Mr. Grounds had left them to fend for themselves. Memories of Billy are painful. Vira feels his presence and hears his voice everywhere. In an effort to retain her last shred of sanity; Vira decides to move the family.

As dusk falls one night, the pitiful little band of five disheveled, half-starving, ragged children, and a sad, weary mother who had been widowed too early, tied their bundles of clothing together. They take what small possessions they can carry, and set out on foot to find a new home. They have nothing. No money, no means of earning a living, no family waiting to greet them with open arms, no idea of what lies ahead in Bath, St. Thomas where they are headed. The uncle and brother-in-law, along with his friends and allies in the community have turned against her, blaming her for Billy's death and for leaving the body of their beloved brother and friend in the hands of strangers. They are so happy to see them go that even as they hurry out of the place which had been so unkind to them, they are not allowed to leave in peace. Their enemies run into their homes, bringing out pots and pans, knocking on them like drums, singing, rejoicing, and shouting at their backs, as they chase the crying family out of their district. Glad to be rid of the Starcky family.

"Then shall he say to those on his left hand.
Be gone from me you cursed into the eternal fire prepared for the devil and his angels.

For I was hungry and you gave me no food, I was thirsty and you gave me nothing to drink…and he will reply to them, solemnly I

declare to you, in so far as you failed to do it for the least of these my children, you failed to do it to me."
Matthew 25: 41-45 (AKJV)

**Life Question:** *Being born poor is not a crime. Being abused as a defenseless child is not a disgrace and will never be held against you. Being a black, poor, abused, wretched, fatherless child is neither a disgrace nor a crime, and will not be laid to your charge. What it does is create opportunities for the scums of the earth that preys on the defenselessness of women and children, who in their distresses depend upon them for protection and support. Where is God when the cries of the poorest and most under privileged escaped their lips begging for relief and deliverance from their plight? Are the cries not heard, or is the ears of God open only to the rich, powerful, educated and privileged?*

**Answer:**

# The Odyssey of Survival

## Chapter Three

### HELL ON EARTH

From Mount Felix to Bath, St. Thomas is a distance of some eighty miles. They travel on foot, forging their way through dense bushes, walking, and walking, unsure of the correct direction. For 5 days and nights they walk, sleeping in the woods, eating what they find in the fields they pass through. Their survival is a miracle. The children are afraid of the dark, jumping at every strange sound whether it's a broken twig or the cries of creatures of the night. Huddled together they comfort one another. Bathing and drinking from the rivers, they keep walking barefoot, exhausted. Five days later they arrive in Bath.

Vira asks for and receives directions to the Seventh Day Adventist Church. Billy had been a member of the denomination, and had introduced her to the religion. At the church they meet the pastor. At the first sight of the dirty, starving, disheveled, weary group, the pastor immediately invites them in. He listens to their story, calls his wife who escorts them to their home. There they are fed, given a change of clothes and beds. But charity does not last forever. Vira has to find a way to provide some semblance of normalcy for her family. By this time the children understand that Daddy is gone forever. His death has thrown them into abject poverty. They own nothing except what's on their backs. No one knows where they are, and no one cares. Vira had not formed friendships nor had she kept in contact with her family. The brood of six is alone in the world dependent upon the mercies of others and of God, to whom Vira cries nightly for deliverance.

Unsure about what kind of arrangement had been made but unable to do any better the family moves into a poor excuse for a house. The roof leaks and the walls have holes in them, but the dirt floor had been so tightly packed that when swept it almost shines. They share one room; Vira and the younger children sleep on the bed with its sagging dried grass filled crocus bag mattress, out of which poke stems which irritates their skin and interrupt their sleep. But it's better than sleeping on the dirt floor. The older children sleep under the table, making that their bedroom. A sheet is draped over the table, which hangs over the sides, providing privacy and some seclusion. The outhouse is dark and stinks, rife with roaches and insects. The congregation of Seventh Day Adventist Church takes pity on them. The wives offer cooked meals and hand-me-down cloths and the husbands offer produce from their fields. The children begin attending school, slowly learning how to write their names, read and do simple arithmetic. Of course there is a price to pay for all this generosity. The debased animal instincts of men find pleasure in the misery of those who need their kindness and mercy the most.

Jamaica is famous for its beautiful idyllic summer days, and romantic nights. Tourists flock the island to bask in its beauty, soak up its sunshine, and sway to the soul stirring melody of reggae, jazz, calypso and every other type of music. But when you are living in abject poverty, beautiful surroundings are totally lost on you. There is no time to stop and smell the roses, no time to lie on the beach and enjoy the clouds and salty wind blowing in your hair. The ocean and rivers are viewed as a source of getting food or for the bathing and washing of clothes, so much energy is expelled in simply getting from one day to the next alive, that beauty goes unnoticed. Much to the children's delight, they are invited to accompany Mr. Smitten and family, one of their benefactors, to the Botanical Garden on a Sunday afternoon. They have no idea what a botanical garden is but the prospect of escaping their hovel for a few hours excites them. After enjoying a picnic lunch with the family the husband generously offers to show Amelia around the garden. She skips along with him to see more of this beautiful place, filled with flowers of all types, butterflies, mazes and secret places.

## The Odyssey of Survival

Amelia and Victoria have become easy targets for rape and abuse. Something has to be done before they end up dead or pregnant. The girls become each other's protector finding ways to secure and protect themselves from these men. Victoria, the braver of the two decides to confide in their mother about what has been happening. Maybe Vira can help stop the abuse. Victoria tells her. To her dismay instead of mother becoming indignant, confronting the men who had been raping her daughters, she turns against them. Vira tells Victoria that she did not believe that any of the good men who had been so kind to them would do such a thing.

"Even if what you say is true, then it is your fault for flaunting yourselves before them or being rude to the people who had been so kind to us. I don't want to hear any more of this sort of thing. Both of you go to your bed, as a punishment for suggesting such awful lies you are getting no dinner and I'm going to teach you a lesson for lying."

Grabbing a whip she beats them then washes out their mouths with soap. Where had they heard about such things? She will have to speak to the teachers at school. This is the first and only time Vira is approached with a problem by her children. Is Vira really unaware of what has been happening to her daughters? Does she care more about a piece of yam, a bunch of bananas, a pound of flour, sugar or corn meal, than she does about her daughters? They need her. They need her to stand in the gap for them, to defend and protect them, to put a stop to the humiliations. Instead Vira buries her head in the sand, feigning ignorance leaving her daughters to the mercy of others. They are defenseless against the men who want to use them to satisfy their sexual desires. Vira has her own way of providing what she can for her family. Many days the children are sent outside to play while one of the good men from church visits with their mother. Huddled together under the house, which stands on stakes, they listen to the squeezing of the grass mattress, as Vira entertains her visitor. The visitors are all men from the church who have come to see how the family is doing or what else can be done to provide for their needs.

# The Odyssey of Survival

One day Amelia feels a strange new sensation in her stomach followed by a sharp pain in her lower abdomen. What is that? She wonders. What caused that pain? Maybe it's the chicken back from last night's dinner. I know it tasted bad and was slimy. The pain persists and then comes a feeling of wetness between her legs. Rushing to the outhouse she quickly pulls down her underwear to investigate. She is shocked at the sight of blood on her panties.

"Oh my God; what happened? What am I going to do now?"

Amelia is thirteen years old. She had never learned anything about this phenomenon. She knows nothing about her body. She has no idea where babies come from, but she had learned one lesson very well: Stay away from men, they only want to stick their huge organs between her legs, pump away on top of her until they shuddered leaving white foam on her. She knows the pain they cause her, how she has to 'walk wide' for days after each encounter. Since turning twelve she had begun formulating a plan. As soon as she is old enough, perhaps when she turns thirteen, she is going to run away. This life of poverty and being held down by men is not even fit for a dog. There is no one to help her so she has to look out for herself. There is just one small problem. Constantly she muses.

"Where do I run to?"

Her instincts tell her that as she matures she will be in greater danger around these men. Run away she must. Wherever she end up can't be worse than if she remains here. Her mind is fixed. In her ignorance about her body, her bleeding throws her into a panic. She flees to the river where she sits in the water, hoping to wash away the blood. Hours pass but still she sits, because each time she notices the water around her gets clear, she gets up, takes a few steps and its back, running down her legs. She sits and cries. No one comes to help her and the blood keeps coming. The sun begins going down over the horizon. She has to go home. Slowly she drags her feet down the hill towards home with blood starting to stream down her legs again. Victoria sees her coming and runs to meet her.

# The Odyssey of Survival

"Where have you been all day? Mama is going to kill you. She's been looking for you all day."

"I don't know what happened," she tells her sister, "but look blood has been coming out of me. Something must have bust in me."

Victoria takes one look at her sister and exclaims. "Nothing bust in you silly. It's your period."

"My what?"

"Your period. It's going to come every month for the rest of your life."

"What are you talking about? Where did you learn about such a thing?"

"From watching mama through the keyhole; I notice that every month about the same time she is bleeding, and she puts on baby nappies to stop the blood from running down her legs. Don't you see nappies on the clothesline and Leroy stop wearing them? That is what she uses them for. And Nancy was telling me the other day that her mother tells her that when she go to the bathroom and see blood on her panties she should come and tell her because her period will start coming. Her mother tells her that for one week every month, for the rest of her life it will come. Her mother also tells her that if she allows boys to mess with her and the blood doesn't come it's because she is going to have a baby. Come on. Let me fix you up."

Retrieving a pillowcase Victoria tears it to pieces making a big pad, which she places between Amelia's legs. Then she tears a string attaches it to the pad, and ties it around her sister's waist to keep the cloth in place. "There you go this will keep you from bleeding all over the place." Amelia looks down at the wad between her legs. She is glad for a solution to her problem but does it have to be so tight? "Thanks sis, but this string is so tight it feels like it's going to cut me in half." Victoria surveys her handiwork and is satisfied with the job. Brushing Amelia's hand away she instructs her.

"Leave it alone it has to be tight or it will fall off you. Do you want everyone to see that you are bleeding?"

With that Amelia resigns herself to her fate. The string around her waist is so tight she thinks her body will be severed in half. For three days Amelia wears the same dirty, blood soaked pad. It's taken off daily, carefully laid aside while she showers, then put right back on. Day in and day out she wears the stinking piece of rag.

On the third day Vira stands over Amelia combing her hair to send her off to school. She sniffs at Amelia, and then sniffs again.

"Did you bathe this morning?" she asked.

"Yes," she replied.

"Then why do you stink? I tell you to take a bath every day. Go bathe, and hurry up so you are not late for school."

Amelia takes another bath, but no amount of bathing can diffuse the stench of three-day-old blood. By this time the pad is black. But she knows no better. Amelia returns from her second bath and her mother resumes combing her hair. Vira's nostrils flare.

"What is wrong with you? Why do you stink so badly? Come here. Lift up your arms let me smell your armpit. Lift up the other one. Open your legs."

The stench, which wafted from between Amelia's legs almost, knocks her to the ground.

"My God, what is *wrong* with you?" she exclaims as she yank down Amelia's underwear.

# The Odyssey of Survival

Utterly humiliated Amelia stands there as her mother take in the sight of the disgusting rag held in place by an equally dirty string. And so Vira discovers that her daughter had begun her menstruation. She huffs away from her returning and throwing her another piece of rag to stuff between her legs. In disgust mother admonishes daughter to take off the filthy rag and replace it with a clean one. Her sex education consists of.

"Now you can go and have boys fool around with you."

"What does that mean? How can boys fool around with me and what does that have to do with what Victoria had called, period?"

There are no answers, because there is no parent to ask for clarification. No boys fool around with her, but the men continue raping her. How Amelia doesn't get pregnant is a mystery. The girls don't get pregnant, but their mother certainly does. Within fourteen months of Vira's husband death the children notice that their mother's stomach is getting bigger, but pays no attention. The details elude them for they are so used to seeing her pregnant and have no concept of how a baby got into a woman's stomach. A few months later, another baby girl is born into the family. She was named Patricia Verona Starcky. The same name as the late husband's five other children. Is this child a product of the deceased husband? Have Billy paid Vira conjugal visits from the grave?

"Thus says the Lord that made thee, and formed thee from the womb, which will help thee.
Fear not, O Jacob my servant, and thou Jeshunn, whom I have chosen.
For I will pour water upon him that is thirsty, and floods upon the dry ground; I will pour my spirit upon thy seed, and my blessings upon your offspring.
And they shall spring up as among the grass, as willows by the water courses."
Isaiah 44:2-4

# The Odyssey of Survival

**Life Question:** *Life, with its twists and turns, ups and downs, can hold us in such tight vices that we feel as if the very last breath is being squeezed out of our lungs. In both the human and animal kingdoms, survival is for the fittest. But how do you become fit enough to survive the iron jaws of the enemy. When a defenseless antelope is held between the jaws of a lioness, can he shake himself free? Or should he say his prayers and give up the ghost silently, dying with dignity and respect intact? Should these young girls remain in the home that is exposing them to continually being raped, and if they don't, what will become of them?"*

*Answer:*

## *Chapter Four*

## TRAGEDY OF TRAGEDIES

A few months after the birth of Patricia, a new man enters the picture. He resides with his common-law wife in the community. Frequent visits turn into overnight rendezvous within the leaky tar and shackle walls of the overcrowded shack, which already houses a mother and six children. With another body there is not enough space or oxygen in the overcrowded room. When he spends the night, all six children sleep under the table. A sheet is used as a make shift door, separating the adults from impressionable children.

Austin Macaroon is a handsome man who had relocated from St. Catherine, another parish on the island. It's rumored that he has fled St. Catherine to avoid supporting the six children he fathered there. To avoid detection he changes his name. The man formerly known as Aubrey Claymont is now Austin Macaroon.

With the new relationship in full swing Vira prepares his daily meals, including hot lunches. These lunches have to be taken to him at his place of employment. Vira delegates the job to Amelia, oblivious of the dangers to which she is prone as she walks the countryside alone. Amelia is entrusted with the food carrier, which she walks five miles to deliver. Leaving home is the highlight of her day, and she makes these treks as pleasant as possible, skipping and hopping along her way. She is still vulnerable to the men, who prey on young girls, but now she is able to outrun most of them; she just has to remain alert.

In small communities gossip travels fast, and before long the woman with whom Austin lives becomes privy to the fact he has formed another relationship. She is not happy. What is she going to do if the unthinkable happens? What if he leaves her for another

## The Odyssey of Survival

woman and not just another woman, but one who has six children of her own? What is he thinking? Has he forgotten that he fled the responsibilities of his own six children? Why on earth would he saddle himself with a brood of snotty nosed, fatherless, poverty stricken, abused children? She is not going to allow this to happen. She will, at any cost, protect her home. Both women are in need of a man. Both of them want this man. Austin is definitely fresh blood and he is probably one of the few unmarried men around. Both women are willing to fight for what they want. They have several confrontations in the streets, in the market, wherever their paths cross. In the meantime Austin enjoys the meals and comforts of both women. On one of his visits to Vira he tries to contribute to the household finances. With one of his charming smiles, he sticks his hand in his pocket, pulls it out and hands her some money. With a smile on her face Vira stretches out her hand to receive the badly needed funds. The smile freezes on her face as she looks at what he has placed in her palm. To her astonishment, there lies a shining coin worth a whopping twenty-five pennies. She is furious. Slowly raising her eyes from her hand she shoots daggers at him. Screaming...

"What do you take me for? What am I supposed to do with this? Do you think this pittance can feed you for a week?"

The smile slowly ebbs from his face, replaced with embarrassment.

"Ah ...I'm sorry I thought it was enough. I'm just trying to help you out knowing that things are hard."

Lifting her left arm high over her head she flings the coin as far away as she can. She spins around on her heels; walks into her home slamming the door in his face. Amelia, witnessing this display, runs off to find the coin. She spends days searching the bushes, but the treasure is lost.

## The Odyssey of Survival

Austin is not a rich man, but that is not the issue, he is a man, and is therefore worth fighting over. And fight they do. Vira decides that she was no longer willing to share him. She wants him to be a father to her fatherless children. After he stayed away from her for two days, she decides the time has come for her to claim what belongs to her. Marching to his home, she pounds on the door demanding he comes out to her. The other woman emerges ordering her off her property. Vira has no intentions of leaving without what she has come to collect. She wants Mr. Macaroon, and is here to issue the last notice to his woman to leave him alone. The other woman has the same intention, to keep what is hers. This dispute can only be settled one way. A heavyweight championship fight is brewing, the prize, a man, not just any man; this is a battle for the only eligible bachelor for miles around. He is willing to become father to six children and a woman who desperately needs a provider. Like a lioness protecting her cubs, she rises to the challenge. Vira's words hold a warning.

"I am warning you, leave him alone. He is mine now. You are not woman enough to keep your man at home, so he came to me. Keep your dirty filthy hands off him. If you don't leave him alone you will be sorry."

"He is mine. We have been together for over one year and were happy until you showed up. You are going to leave him alone if it means that I have to beat your ass."

They fight. What a sight, two grown women getting into a fistfight over a man. Like the cats they are, blows fly through the air, hitting and scratching, yelling and cussing at each other. They pull hair and clothes and fight some more. When the dust settled only the winner is left standing. Vira wins. Vira has literally torn the cloths off the other woman's back leaving her trying desperately to cover her nakedness with pieces of rags hanging from her shoulders. The community stands by watching as this drama unfolds. Her children have barely been able to hold their heads up but now the ground holds special interest as they walk around.

# The Odyssey of Survival

It has been bad enough being labeled the poorest in the district. Now they have another stigma attached to them.

Where is Austin during all of this? What does he have to say about which woman he loves and whom he wants to be with? He is given no choice in the matter. When he returns from work at the end of the day, Vira informs him that he now belongs to her and is never to be seen with the other woman again. His pleadings fall on deaf ears; he is not even allowed to return to his former home to collect his belongings. She strides over to the house demanding his clothing. They are thrown out the door. Vira proudly picks up each piece, tucking them under her arms, walking away hearing the snickers behind her. At home she hangs them over the only chair in the shack. Vira controls every aspect of Austin's life. Money is very important to her, and to his embarrassment she begins showing up at his place of employment on Friday afternoons, going directly to the foreman of the carpenter shop, collecting his pay. If he is lucky he will be given one pound every two weeks for his personal use. If at anytime she feels the need for additional funds, he has to give it up or give her a good reason why it had been spent. He has no idea what he had gotten himself into. If he thought life with his six children was hard, the noose around his neck has now been tightened a hundred fold, leaving just enough room for his finger to wiggle around, relieving the pressure from his Adam's apple. Eventually, the embarrassment becomes too much for the beaten woman to bear. Vira goes out of her way to flaunt her victory in her face. The district is too small for two lionesses to reign, so the beaten woman packs up her belongings and moves out of the area. The community ostracizes Vira because the residents do not agree with her actions. She doesn't care. She has forgotten their kindness to her and her children. Now with a man to call her-own she no longer needs them. The visitations stop, and the girls get a reprieve from having to beg for food and pay with their bodies.

Soon she is fighting with Austin. During a loud verbal fight, Vira grabs a machete and with precision, chops him squarely in his forehead. He reels from the shock of the blow, falling backward, as blood spouts from the open wound, blinding his eye.

# The Odyssey of Survival

The eye literally pops out of its socket as he flies into the bushes; yelling for help.

"Lawd mi dead now! Help! Somebody help me! Mi eye Lawd mi can't see. Help!"

No help comes from Vira or from anyone else. He wails like a wounded animal dashing through the bushes, trying to find relief from the pain in his face. Back and forth he runs, begging for help. With arms folded across her chest Vira remain aloof to his suffering, closing her ears against his wailing. Desperately he tries to save his sight protecting it with his hand. He disappears into the bushes. Hours later he emerges, bloody and crazed with pain. The children huddle together crying at the awful sight they witness. Vira tells them to shut up or they also will receive a beating. Then she walks away, ignoring Austin's cries. The girls do their best to clean the wound. To everyone's surprise, the wound heals and his eye is not lost, but he will go to his grave wearing his scar like a badge of honor.

Life at home becomes a little easier for the children for at least now there was a male figure in the home who provide for them. At times the older girls find themselves being molested by the men in the neighborhood. For the most part they are left alone, not so much out of respect for the new head of the household, but because they had witnessed how vicious their mother can be. Pity she will not fight for her own flesh and blood. Animals of prey seek out the youngest, weakest and most vulnerable of the herd on which to inflict harm. In this family, all the children are weak. Almost everyone has been abused, molested, raped or beaten mercilessly. Vira was the perpetrator, and when she was not administering backbreaking blows she closed her eyes, turning her back or just feign ignorance at the plight of her offspring.

Carelessly Vira allows Victoria to accompany Mr. Wantsome, a neighbor on a four-day trip. He was one of the few men who had helped them without helping himself to them. With no supervision, no one to hear her cries she is at his mercy. Far away from home they bed down in a strange place on the first night of their sojourn. Playing the part of a concerned neighbor, he fusses about. What Victoria does not know is that she has bedded down with the enemy. Just at the moment when she makes the final shuffle, shifting her body into a comfortable position as sleep makes her eyelids heavy, she feels the first touch on her leg. She experiences no fear and simply draws her legs tighter under her body. The touch comes again, not fleeting but lingering, intentional. Her senses tell her this is no accident. "What is he doing?" His hand caresses her chest searching for her breast. Her body stiffens as the probing hand begins a slow roaming of her body, this time stroking her leg in a suggestive manner. Petrified, she sits up in bed, holding the thin sheet up to her chin, seeking protection from the evil about to befall her. In no uncertain gesture, he yanks the sheet from her weak fingers as she shuffles back, hitting the head of the bed with her body. Like an animal in heat he pursues her, cornering her when there was no more room to flee. Memories of the other men who had violated her in the past, race through her mind. This one she trusted, he had been around them for months and had made no attempt to be anything except a good friend to the family. But apparently he had only been waiting for the right moment to present itself. And here it is. His strong arms quickly overpower her and he throws her back onto the bed. Loudly she cries, begging him not to carry out his intentions. But her cries for mercy seem to ignite his passion. Weakly she fights back knowing he will win this battle. As he prepares to imbed himself into her, he does something which completely confuses her. Instead of doing what she had become accustomed to, he flips her over onto her stomach. What is he doing? Was he going to leave her alone after all? For a moment she hopes so until his hands begun separating the cheeks of her buttocks. She fights and screams but he holds her firmly in place, pressing her face down into the sheets muffling her cries. With burning persistence he lunges and forces himself into her anus. The pain of rape was still fresh in her mind but this is worse than the hymen of her virgin body being ripped away. This cannot be happening but it was. She was being raped in her anus.

"No, please stop it, you are hurting me. Stop it! What are you doing? No stop it. Somebody help me."

# The Odyssey of Survival

Her pleas fall on deaf ears.

"If you keep still it won't hurt so much. Stop fighting and keep still. It will be over before you know it."

"Noooo!" She screams as with one final thrust he plunges, imbedding himself into her anus.

Roughly he continues pulling back and pressing himself into her body. Victoria feels the hot rods of fire piercing her flesh. Death was welcome. Her muscles rebel but he didn't care about her pain. He is enjoying himself. Her body finally relents, relaxing under great pressure, helping her to withstand the pain being inflicted on her. From past experiences, she remembers that lying still causes the pain to be more bearable, so she grabs hold of the sheets, makes a ball out of them hugging them to herself. She buries her face in its folds as she succumbs to the onslaught of pain ripping through her with every thrust.

Satisfied, Mr. Wantsome rolls himself from her back where he had straddled her. Lying on his back, eyes closed in the aftermath of sexual satisfaction. With swollen eyes Victoria peers at him. How could he have done this to her? She had trusted him. The other men who had abused her and her sisters were pigs. But they had gotten to know this one. He lives next door and had slept in her mother's bed after having sex with her mother. She knows all about them by peeking behind the curtain and pretending to be asleep at nights when he came over. She had seen him huffing and puffing on top of her mother. How could he have done this to *her*? She had hoped that he would have been the one to replace her own dead father. Movement is impossible. For a long time after he had finished with her she lays there. No words have been spoken, no threats made about repercussions if she told her mother, he must have known she would not be believed, so why bother telling her to keep her mouth shut. He simply falls asleep. Listening to his snores, she sniffles, crying, wondering what to do. They have two more nights to spend together in this place. What was she going to do? Her actions for the remainder of the trip didn't matter. Behaving rudely, ignoring his instructions during the day and making a pest of herself don't elicit the response she so desperately desires. Instead of becoming upset with her, punishing and leaving her alone, he keeps his nightly rendezvous with her, repeating the anal rape. Stripping her of the small amount of dignity she has left. She sullenly obeys his commands, knowing that obedience shortens the time and intensity of the assaults. The trip is finally over and she returns home. She confides in Amelia. Huddled together in a corner away from the eyes and ears of Vira and Austin, she recounts what had happened to her. The question uppermost in their minds put fear in their hearts; if her experience was any indication of the nature of the beast living next door to them; they had just stepped into a fate worse than death. Their mother trusted him, frequently asking him to watch them when she was away from home. Was he going to be their regular rapist? Did he plan to prey on them? Would their mother step forward and protect them from this animal?

"When the poor and needy seek water, and there is none, and their tongue fails for thirst, I the Lord will hear them, I the God of Israel will not forsake them.
I will open rivers in high places, and fountains in the midst of the valleys; I will make the wilderness a pool of water, and the dry land springs of water.
I will plant in the wilderness the cedar of Shittah tree, and the myrtle, and the oil tree; I will set in the desert the fir tree, and the pine tree, and the box tree together.
That they may see and know, and consider, and understand together, that the hand of the Lord hath done this, and the Holy One of Israel hath created it."
Isaiah 41: 17-20 (KJV)

**Life question:** *Nothing should be more important to a mother than the protection of her children. When parents neglect these responsibilities leaving children to suffer at the hands of unscrupulous men, should they be held accountable for the crimes committed? In today's society would this mother be tried and found guilty for neglect and playing a part in the molestation of her children? And what about these poor wretched girls, how will they survive? What should they have done?*

*Answer:*

## *Chapter Five*

## ALLIANCE WITH THE DEVIL

It's a balmy Thursday evening at about 6:30 pm, on August 1st 1957, in the Morant Bay hospital, that a beautiful baby girl makes her entrance into the world. She is the daughter of Vira Starcky and Austin Macaroon. She weighs in at a whopping 10 pounds, breaking the hospital's scale as she is placed on it. She opens her mouth letting out her first cry. Her mother takes an instant dislike to her and her father falls in love.

After weeks of disagreement about the naming of his precious baby (Austin wants to name his daughter Catherine), Vira wins the argument and she is named Marcia Elaine. This is where I enter the picture, the first child of their union. I am the product of a man for whom my mother fought and a mother, who hates, neglects and abuses her children. My older siblings tell me of my mother's constant beatings of me as a child; and my father's attempts to defend me. Maybe she blames me for the life they created. The noose around her neck must have gotten a bit tighter with the appearance of another child. Life could not have promised much hope for a poor woman who has now given birth to eleven children, with seven to care for. Frustration and anger must have been her constant companions as she trudged through her daily toils. And so my mother despises me and my father loves me. He tries his best to protect me from unnecessary whippings, but he has to work, the family has to be provided for and so like all the other children I am at my mother's mercy.

# The Odyssey of Survival

We continue living in St. Thomas, but the address changes to a larger place, making the accommodations for the growing family more acceptable. While Daddy works Vira never stops looking for ways to improve the lot of her little flock. Even in her harsh treatment of us a tiny thread to make us better, runs deep within her. In her inability to provide for us she turns to others. Help has a strange way of coming with a price tag; at times the price listed on the tag far exceeds the value. One price, which should never be paid by anyone, is the sacrifice of children for a few dollars or a bag of food. Unfortunately, that became our legacy.

Mother forms a friendship with a man who demands payment in the highest and most reprehensible form; her daughters. As the years pass, one by one we are taken to the altar and offered up as sacrifices to the devil clad in a suit, sitting in a big house on the hill, serving his country from one of the highest positions in the land. How mother met and formed an alliance with the most powerful man in the district of St. Thomas remains a mystery. Vira Stackey, and the mayor, who ran for political office and is elected as the government representative for St. Thomas are best friends. The alliance is so strong, that he is named as my godfather.

Two years after my birth, Bridget Pansy is born into the family. She is followed by Alicia Janice who is followed by Cheryl Anita. Gregory Anthon Alistair is the last of the bunch of Starcky/Macaroon children. Vira began giving birth at the age of sixteen. The first surviving child, Amelia was born to her at the age of nineteen, the last child at the age of forty-one years old. Is it any wonder that mother is angry and bitter, after twenty- five years of baby production? Even the finest machine comes to a screeching halt from its constant usage and production. None of us escaped the wrath of a woman who apparently had never known the love of her mother, had no time to love herself, nor had she formed any type of lasting friendships with neighbors. She has never experienced the life changing love of Jesus, although she regularly attends church and is very strict in the traditions of her beliefs. We are a sad, abused, pitiful bunch who finds love and comfort with one another. At the time of my birth Amelia was fourteen years old and had already run away from home. She could no longer withstand the sexual, physical, and emotional abuse and decided to make it on her own. What could happen to her out there that had not happened at home? Where could she possibly end up that was worse than home?

Victoria follows Amelia, leaving home looking for a better life. Most of the other children have been given away to others who continue the abuse. Lester and Leroy had been given to a carpenter who promised to teach them the business. Lynnette is given to a teacher who continues the emotional abuse of her mother, scarring her for life. Patricia who is two years my senior remains at home. My first memory of home is at about five years old. Bridget and I have contracted whooping cough. Locked in the house, forbidden to play outside, we pass our time between bouts of coughing looking out the window at the others playing in the warm sunshine. On the third day of our isolation we notice our father returning home carrying an animal by its tail. We almost fall out the window, as we lean forward to see what strange creature he carries Mother sees him coming, and rushes out to inquire.

Stopping in her tracks she yells, "What are you doing with that filthy field rat?"

"I'm going to make rat soup for the girls; a woman in the market told me that it's the cure for whooping cough."

"You must be mad." mother retorted. "Take that dirty thing out of my yard."

Daddy persists. Do you prefer that they die? Don't you hear how bad they sound especially at nights?"

Holding up the bunch of bushes in her hand she explains. "I am going to boil them some bush tea. Let the dirty rat go. Are you crazy?"

## The Odyssey of Survival

"But this will work faster than any bush tea. Everybody in the market tells me that that's what they give to their children when they have whopping cough."

Getting angrier by the minute she explodes.

"Man, get that filthy thing out of my yard! And you had better not let it go here so it can come into the house. Over my dead body are you going to make rat soup in this house. Get out of here you stupid man."

Dejected, Daddy returns to the field; where he disposes of the rat. That was one occasion, (maybe the only one), for which we are glad Mother stood up to Daddy.

Country life can be peaceful. Times can be hard. People are poor. There are no modern amenities. But life is simple. Expenses are the bare minimum. Food is grown in the fields or in the backyard. Animals are raised and used for the feeding of the family, and children are supposed to be free to run and play, growing up strong and healthy. But country life is also dangerous. Illiteracy is high and tempers flare quickly. Heads of men can be chopped off at the slightest provocation, and much to the chagrin of the relatives left behind, the murderer likely remains free if just cause for the murder is found. Families are large because parents have nothing else to do at night but make babies. As soon as a woman weans a baby, she conceives again. Our family of eleven children is large but not unique. The blending of families is quite common, because men are likely to die at an early age, either due to accidents or to the unavailability of immediate medical care. The difference between our family and others is the open hostility our mother displays towards us. She has given birth to fifteen children, eleven of whom have survived. After her losses she might have thanked God for each child that is born healthy and survived, but instead she grows more resentful toward each one, almost to the point of blaming the innocent babies for their existence. Mother constantly tells me how she "Wished she had pulled my tongue out at birth and killed me." I live in constant fear of this threat being carried out. To make it harder for her; I keep my tongue firmly between the shackles

## The Odyssey of Survival

of my teeth. Up to my age of seven years, we lived in St. Thomas. One day our parents pack up our belongings load them in a truck, help us up into the truck, and tell us to go to sleep. We are moving. The truck rolls out onto the dirt road, leaving our little home behind. "Where are we going?" we quietly ask one another, wide eyed with fear and excitement. Mother tells us to be quiet, but offers one bit of information. "Go to sleep the lot of you, we are moving to Kingston, that's the big city. When you wake up in the morning we'll be there. Now I don't want to have to talk to any of you again, close your eyes and go to sleep." We are going on an adventure. Valiantly we try to be quiet as we watch the countryside pass by. We want to see everything, but it's a long trip and soon one, by one, our eyelids droop, and we are off to sleep dreaming of life in the big city. We enjoyed the adventure. We are moving to the city.

A day later, tired but excited, we arrive. Our parents unpack our belongings and we explore the new surroundings. Everything looks different. Instead of bushes and dirt roads we see buildings and paved streets. The bathroom and kitchen are located inside the house. It's a big house, the biggest we had ever seen. Our eyes pop out when we see all the bedrooms; all two of them. Instantly we fall in love with our new home at number three Paradise Street, Kingston, Jamaica.

Across the street from our new home is a huge building surrounded by wire fence. "What is that?" we ask Daddy. That is the Mental Health Sanitarium, called Bellevue Asylum. In other words, it's a madhouse where all the mad people are locked up." He replies. At one end of the street is the ocean and we are in heaven. Life takes on a new meaning. We are happy, have more freedom and for the first time we begin feeling like human beings. Daddy gets hired as the carpenter at the Children's Hospital, and the older children and I begin attending school. On Sunday mornings Daddy takes all of us down to the beach for a swim. We frolic in the warm waters, build sand castles, while soaking up the radiant sunshine. Returning home to hot Johnnycakes with ackee and salt fish; washed down with hot chocolate tea. After breakfast we ran outside to play.

# The Odyssey of Survival

For pennies we buy balls sold over the high walls of the asylum. We throw our pennies over the wall and the balls are tossed to us. We hear voices belonging to faces we saw peering through the holes as they peddled their wares from their place of confinement. In the large backyard, one Sunday evening, while we were playing with a newly purchased ball, we notice that the cords had begun to unravel. As it comes apart in our hands we are fascinated to discover the inward makings of the ball. The last bit of string falls away, revealing tightly rolled newspaper. From this wad an unpleasant odor assails our nostrils. What's on the inside? Gingerly we rip into the newspaper. Before long we are looking at the core of the ball; a load of human waste. Screaming, we toss the vile object as far away as we can. Our screams bring Daddy outside. We tell him of our discovery. He chuckles…

"What do you expect? You bought it from madmen in an asylum."

There ended our patronage of the wares over the wall. We begin attending church on a regular basis. Vira's first husband Billy was a member of the Seventh-day Adventist Church. (S.D.A). She had learned about the denomination through him and had experienced kindness from members of the faith after his death. When she traveled to St. Thomas the SDA church had taken her in. Mother had never forgotten how generous they had been to her and her children and although never baptized she considered herself a member of the faith. Daddy, on the other hand had never heard of the SDA church. He had grown up in the Anglican faith worshipping on Sunday. Of course this caused great conflict, but mother won. The household attends church on Saturday. Mother and Daddy have been in a relationship for ten years, and have five children together. The church frowns upon the common-law household. To become members of this religious sect, our parents need to get married.

On June 8th, 1966, a beautiful Saturday evening, our parents exchanged wedding vows in the North Street S.D.A Church. Mother is ecstatic; she looks radiant in a calf length white bridal dress.

# The Odyssey of Survival

A shoulder length veil covers her head and she carries a bunch of delightful white flowers. Daddy is stunningly handsome in a cream suit. The children are all decked out in finery and fearing the beating we have been warned will be forthcoming for any misbehavior, we display perfect manners. The reception following the ceremony is a fun affair. The church outdid itself, providing, food, drink and a very enjoyable and memorable day. The following afternoon, both our parents are baptized in the same church. Everyone rejoices. The family is now official members of the Seventh Day Adventist denomination. We are constantly on the move, either because of problems with the neighbors (my mother lives peacefully with no one), or because the neighborhood wakes up to find a female neighbor hanging from a mango tree in the front yard. Each move means a new school with its own new set of problems. But our parents do not think about the importance of maintaining some type of stability for their children's education. We are unceremoniously yanked out of school every year. We learn not to form friendships, remaining aloof from our counterparts and peers. One day Daddy sits us down and tells us that we have six older brothers and sisters. He explains the family dynamics and that a couple of his other children want to meet his new family. Mother, of course is furious, but Daddy is determined not to allow her to bully him into abandoning his children again. Two weeks later Daddy comes home with a tall young man proudly dressed in the uniform of a police officer.

"This is your brother Ethan."

Shyly we greet him, each one seriously going forward to shake hands introducing ourselves. He stays for dinner and comes by often to visit. We grow to love him as a great big brother. Soon after we meet him, he tells us that he is going to get married. Bridget and I are flower girls. Proudly we smiled for the camera in our yellow dresses and size too large white shoes. After the birth of their daughter, Sasha, Greta, his wife becomes ill. She stays in our home while she recuperates. Over time we meet Daddy's other children, but Ethan, becomes closest to the family.

# The Odyssey of Survival

Dysfunctional, when looked up in the dictionary should mean. "Starcky-Macaroon family". I believe that before the word was coined, our family suited the meaning to perfection. There is no real stability in our lives. We live in constant fear of our mother; her heavy left hand has no mercy. It only metes out punishment. It is never open to a hurt, crying child to run for refuge. Actually the wielding of those arms has hurt the crying child. We have no contact with our grandmother, aunts or other family members. We are allowed to speak with no one; no friend from school or neighbors visit the home. We are strictly commanded to keep no friends at school, no playing after school or idling about. Her philosophy is this:

"There are enough of you to keep one another company. You don't need friends."

We move again, and this time we are living in a house that is too small for the family. There is some type of occupancy restriction and we are over the limit. We have to take turns playing outside; the neighbors cannot know how many of us live here. It's funny at first, but soon we begin feeling like prisoners. Tempers flair easily and the belt rains down on us just as frequently. One day the landlord comes by unexpectedly, too many of us are outside playing. She discovers seven faces peering at her. She asks for our mother.

"Mrs. Macaroon are all these children yours?"

"Yes. All of them are mine."

"When you rented the house I asked you how many children you had and you said five. Now how many do I see six or seven?"

"Not missing a beat", Mother replied.

"You tell me who is going to rent me a house with seven children. What does it matter to you how many of us live in here as long as you get your rent on time. As a matter of fact it's not the first of the month, the rent isn't due yet so what are you doing here?

## The Odyssey of Survival

You are trespassing on my property. I suggest you leave before I call the police."

Mother slams the door in her face signaling the end of the conversation. The only bathroom in the two-room apartment is located upstairs. Two of us sleep on a bed under the stairs. The toilet flushes many times each day. One Friday afternoon while both parents are out of the home, someone flushes the toilet. Instead of the contents smoothly disappearing the bowl fills up with water. The child yells for me to come here now. Running up the stairs I meet water and feces pouring down the stairs. Bridget and I clean up the mess, then we turn our attention to the soaked mattress under the stairs. Pulling it along, walking backwards into the yard. Suddenly excruciating pain shoot through my foot. Screaming, I drop the mattress and grab my foot. To my horror my big toe is almost severed. My screams bring the neighbor running to investigate. Seeing the bloody toe hanging by skin, she quickly ties my foot with a towel stemming the blood flow. Daddy comes home and takes me to the hospital where Tetanus shots, stitches and weeks of hobbling along preceded my healing. The toilet continues overflowing. It becomes as much a way of life as running to the ice truck to get bits of ice chips to cool our thirst.

One day Janice did not come home from school, after intensely searching for her we find her wandering the streets. A young girl had stolen her lunch then enticed her to follow her home. The girl disappeared around many corners, leaving Janice confused and lost. Mother takes no part in the search. Getting rid of one mouth to feed will be a blessing. She hates the very sight of Janice anyway. My little sister is found and returned safely home. Our parents become aware of a new subdivision being built by the government. A number of the homes will be allocated to families who qualified under a housing program. Mother immediately contacts her influential government friend, my godfather. With his help coupled with Daddy's position at the hospital we become eligible for one of the new homes.

# The Odyssey of Survival

September 9th 1967, is moving day, At long last we are the proud owners of our own home. We are ecstatic. By this time, Amelia and Victoria have migrated to Canada, through a domestic program instituted between the government of Jamaica and Canada.

My godfather who is a Minister of the government, is also the mastermind behind this program, so my older sisters have been included in the migration to Canada. They each have two children before leaving the island; these four children now live with us, making a total of ten children in the home. The new house has two bedrooms and one bathroom, but none of us notice the cramped space for twelve of us. We are very grateful for a house. It's the first place we have had to call our own. No more hiding from landlords, or having to move to another home because the neighbors dislike our mother. Even if they don't get along we have to stick it out. This is our home. Mother's hatred for us grows as we evolve from girls into teenagers. Unlike other parents who proudly smile as their children grow up, she denounces and curses us making us ashamed of our budding bodies. Instead of thanking God that despite all the hardships we endured, we have escaped involvement in drugs or alcohol, or running with the wrong crowd, she threatens to kill us. Her threats to pour hot oil down our ears while we sleep are so real that we live in fear of going to sleep. At night we try taking turns watching over one another. Inevitably sleep takes over, but not before holding pillows tightly over our heads. Physical abuse is one thing, but mental and emotional abuse is an insidious evil. At the hands of my mother we suffer both physical and mental abuse. For as long as I can remember, outside the hearing of our father, we are told over and over again, that we are less than nothing.

"You Mr. Mac pickneys were never wanted. The entire lot of you can go to hell for all I care. Billy is the only husband I ever had. He is the only man I ever loved. Amelia is the only child I ever had and all the rest of you are nothing but garbage. I hate the whole lot of you."

# The Odyssey of Survival

We hang our heads in shame. After a particularly vicious beating, she makes me look in her eyes as she tells me how much she hates me.

"I wish I had pulled your tongue out of your head when you were born and killed you. I hate the sight of you, get out of my sight, you piece of shit."

Then she spits in my face. Spitting in our faces is just another way for her to humiliate us. It is one of the lowest degrees of humiliation, and she has mastered the technique. Bridget is unaware that she is committing a mortal sin, by turning on the television without asking permission. Mother comes up behind her and using the instrument in her hand chops Bridget in her head while screaming at her for touching her prized possession. In fright Bridget spins around, and is met with a wad of spit in her face. We look on in horror.

"Bridget spit back in her face." Janice yells.

"No, she is my mother." Bridget replies.

While blood flows down her face, and stinking spit drips onto her blouse, we help Bridget outside, cleaning her up and comforting her. Bridget sports a hole in the side of her head where mother's stiletto heel lodged itself barely missing her eye when mother threw it at her.

"I can kill any one or the entire bunch of you and get away with it because I have quick-silver in my head and will be diagnosed as crazy. No judge will lock me up in prison because I know all of them."

She is right. For some strange reason she knows and is friendly with the entire police force. They hold her in high esteem. Visiting the home, one officer remarks, "Oh what a lovely lady, she reminds me of my mother. You kids had better listen to your mother, she is a wise woman and will never steer you wrong."

## The Odyssey of Survival

If they only knew the hell we live in. We have no idea what quicksilver in her head is, and tries our best not to find out. The neighborhood children refer to mother as an "obeah woman," further ostracizing us from society. She is feared by all, but by no one as much as those of us living under the same roof with her. Daddy does not escape her wrath; he is berated and cursed every day of the week. At night we lie awake listening to them fight. After he gets dressed one morning the sole of his feet began to itch. By the end of the day his feet are swollen to twice their size. He scratches his feet with everything his hands find. He turns his shoe over, knocking the bottom, to see if an insect had hidden itself in the toes, and white powder flutters in the air. He swears she has worked obeah on him, trying to swell his body until it burst. We have no idea what to believe, each of us run for our shoes, turning them over to loosen whatever could be hidden therein. With extreme caution shoes and clothing are worn. After years of ferocious fighting between our parents, Daddy packs his bags and moves out of his house. Mother finds him and rains terror at the home of the friend who had taken him in. He moves back home. It's a classic case of.

"I don't want you but I would rather see you dead than let someone else have you."

Janice is the most vocal of the lot. She does not suffer silently, but boy does she suffer. She happens to be a shade or two of a darker complexion than the rest of us. The only thing my mother hates more than she hates her children is a black child, and Janice is exposed to double whammy. Mother refers to her as the black one, a black pot, the black monkey and many other derogatory terms. Janice's beatings are merciless. She quietly takes nothing, as the blows rain down and the curse words go up, Janice calls mother every name in the book.

"You are a wicked woman, you are a murderer, and you are going to burn in hell you bitch, murder."

She kicks, slaps, and stomps in her stomach. Janice is beaten to a frazzle. But she is not afraid to retaliate against her. She is rebellious fearing no one. Mother dresses and takes Janice out with her on a Sunday afternoon. We're puzzled; she never takes her any place. When they return Janice receives the worst beating of her life. We look at each other wondering when Mother would stop hitting her. She hits her over the head with a pan, kicks her in the gut, pounces her in the face, back, stomach; she kicks her again and again. Janice is losing the fight, she is rolled up in a ball on the ground, but this did not stop the beatings. We realize that we have to intervene.

    Throwing caution to the wind, Bridget and I run between the blows. We feel them cascading upon our backs and shoulders but we ignore the pain. Rescuing our sister even as mother kicks and spits on us; but we cover Janice with our bodies taking the blows for her. Satisfied, Mother huffs away screaming hateful insults at us. We sink to the floor dissolving into tears. Our lives flash before our eyes as we come close to death's door at the hands of our mother. Why does our mother hate us so much? We have no idea. We come to the realization that our mother is desperately trying to kill us. Our young minds are unable to conceive why our mother wants to be rid of her children. We think parents are supposed to love and care for their children. Of one thing we are sure. We have to come together as one force, drawing strength from and giving strength to one another solely for the sake of our survival. Janice coins the term "murderation." which we use to describe our abuse. Amid our tears, our bruises and our heartaches, we make a pact with one another.

*We will not allow her to kill any one of us. When she begins beating one, she will have to beat all of us, when she curses one; she has to curse all of us. If she sends one to bed with no dinner, we will all go to bed hungry, or we will find ways to sneak food to one another. Somehow we will survive her.* **We are not going to allow her to kill us!**
    Patricia, whom I follow in birth order, also hates us, but she harbors a particular dislike for me. As the oldest child in the home she is responsible for most of the chores. She seeks every opportunity to beat on me, and make me complete her chores along with mine. She is cleaning the house, using red Rexo floor polish and a coconut brush to

polish and shine the terrazzo tiles. She calls me and sends me on an errand.

"Go upstairs and bring me the book which is lying on the bed." I take a step forward and she yells at me.

"Don't walk on the floor that I just cleaned." I check to see if I had grown wings, there is none attached to my back. "How do you expect me to go upstairs without walking on the floor? I can't fly."

Getting in my face she explains. "I'm giving you to the count of ten to go get me my book; if you step on the floor and I see one mark I'm going to whip you. One, two, three…"

I step on the newly polished floor and she punches me, I take another step and she hits me again. Turning around I balled my fist and hit her soundly in the stomach. We fight. I get a sound beating, but that's all right she won't mess with me again. I get another whipping when mother returns home and hears her side of the story.

The Macaroon children are always referred to as Mr. Mac pickneys. Daddy makes no secret of his love for us, which only serve to infuriate mother. Patricia is treated no different from his children, but she deeply resented him and his children. She was only one year old when he entered the patchwork of the family. As far as *I know* he has not done anything to her, but then again, what do I know? Anything could have happened in our family. Mother hates us, Patricia hates us, and we have no contact with our older siblings. Another part of Mother's insidious evil that she perpetrates against us is that she often tells us how her daughter Amelia and the other older children want nothing to do with us. What have we done to make our older sisters and brothers hate us? Daddy cannot protect us from the reign of terror under which we live. He goes off to work daily, not knowing what craziness he will return to at the end of the day. At the slightest provocation, or if Mother gets upset about the tiniest thing done or said by him, when he comes home from work hungry and tired, there is no dinner waiting for him. Her regular practice of inflicting punishment on him is to prepare the evening meal early,

# The Odyssey of Survival

command us to eat our dinner, and then eradicate every indication that a meal had been prepared and eaten. The dishes are washed, the pots scrubbed, the stove cleaned and the floor swept. She commands us to keep our mouths shut about eating dinner. Tearfully we swallow the food, whispering among ourselves about how cruel she is. Daddy has gone to work all day and now he's coming home to nothing to eat. We try saving some of our food for him, but she discovers us and gives the food to the dog.
He comes home tired and waits for his dinner. No scents or sounds come from the kitchen.

"What's going on?" he asked. "No dinner tonight?"

That's the opening she has been waiting for; she lunges at him screaming about his inability to provide for the family. There is no money to buy food. How dare you ask for dinner?" We cry. As soon as it is safe to talk, we tell Daddy about what she made us do and how sorry we are to have eaten without leaving him something to eat. He looks at our tear-stained faces and tells us. "Don't worry; it's not your fault." Slowly he gets up from the table, goes out the door and walks over to the corner shop. There he buys himself a bun and cheese, or a loaf of bread and a can of sardines; not only for him, but enough for all of us. I love my Daddy.

It's my first day of high school. I'm excited, feeling all grown up in my new uniform and shoes. I mingle with the new students, each one seeming more interesting than the one before. The boys seem like men. Will I have a boyfriend by graduation? In my attempts to appear normal I commit the unpardonable sin of talking to strangers. Not only have I spoken and made new friends at school, but, on our walk home we exchange school supplies. I sling her red school bag over my shoulder, while she hugs my new folder to her chest. We fully intend to return each other's stuff at the corner where we part company. I arrive home carrying something that does not belong to me. Only after separating that I discover the mistake. I have no clue about her whereabouts, no idea where she lives.

# The Odyssey of Survival

Mother notices me before I reach the gate. Her piercing eyes notices that I'm carrying a school bag, not a folder. She had not bought me a bag. Only God can help me now.

"Good evening Mama."

Narrowing her eyes she questions me.
"Whose bag is that? Where did you get it from?"

Quaking in my shoes, the explanation forms in my mind but is never uttered.

"Get out of here and don't come back until you find the person to whom that belongs. I sent you to school to learn, not to make friends."

"But." I stammer
"Gal, don't make me kill you tonight. Go find the gal and give her back her bag.

Don't come back until you have what I sent you to school with."

She storms into the house and slams the door behind her. I walk back to the home of three students who attended the same elementary school asking the different girls if they know where Beverly Brown, the new girl at school today lived? No one knows. I wander the streets aimlessly, crying, I don't know what to do. It begins to get dark. I drift back home, bag still in tow. One of my sisters opens the door letting me into the house.

"Did you find the owner of the bag?" Mother bellows.

"No mama, I don't know where she lives, but I'll return it in the morning."

The left hand hidden behind her back flashes forward; holding the dreaded rock steady. A torrent of blows rain down on my head, shoulders, arms and legs with such force that I stagger falling backward. As I fall she kicks me in the stomach stomping on me. Janice and Bridget rush forward, lunging at her; they beg her to stop beating me.

"You are a murderer. Leave my sister alone. You are too wicked."

With a swift blow to their faces and threats to douse them with a pot of boiling water, they are forced to retreat. The beating is vicious. After she has satisfied herself I lay in a bloody pile on the floor whimpering like a wounded animal. Daddy arrives home a few minutes after the blows stopped coming. I am still lying where she left me.
"What have you done to the child?" he demanded "What did she do to make you beat her like this?" He bends down to help me up.

"If you touch her you will get your share." Mother warns.

He continues helping me up. She loses control of herself and a barrage of blows and curse words come down on him. He ignores her paying attention to me. I'm bleeding from my face, arms and legs, and can barely get on my feet from the pain in my stomach. He does his best to help me get cleaned up while comforting me. We both get our beatings that night. With no compassion in any of her bones, she makes me attend school the next day. What a sight I am. The teachers question me about my appearance. I make excuses hiding the tears as best as I can. My mother offers us no love, but our father is warm, loving and kind. He is a little on the stocky side with a balding head, and the soft brown hair around the sides of his head is often being brushed by one of us. His light brown eyes fascinate us when they twinkle with mischief nightly when we gather around him on a canvas cot under the starry sky. He recounts stories of life as a child in the country. He delights in telling us scary stories of ghosts and spirits in the fields, of rolling calves, and all types of strange creatures of the dark. We laugh and are allowed to be children, often too scared to go to sleep after story time. Daddy is a lover of mangos, especially the variety called 'Number Eleven.' It's delicious with its natural sugar and soft textured skin, and an abundance of juice flows freely from the moment your teeth sink into its skin piercing the flesh hidden within. The only problem with these mangos is that, because of their sweetness, they produced worms on the inside when fully ripe. Daddy finds a way to disregard these little invertebrates. He gets himself two or three mangos and waits until its dark. Then he gets himself a plastic bag for the discarded seed, gets a chair and sits outside in the dark and enjoys his mangos. We ask about his behavior and he tells us,

"This is the only way to eat and enjoy mangos. In the dark; where everything tastes good and you can't see anything." We think he's crazy, and while laughing, tell him so. Regardless of what's going on between our parents. Daddy can always be counted on to remember us. At the end of each day he returns home from work with something in his hand or in his pocket for the children. He brings home mangos, apples, pears, plums, and cherries, anything that's in season. If he doesn't have a bag in his hand we know there's something in his pockets. He comes through the gate and we all run to greet him. He stands there with his arms above his head as we ravish through his pockets, searching to find the treasures he brings us. A candy is sufficient. It's not the size or value of what he brings home, it's the fact that he loves us enough to think about us, to make us feel wanted. We are grateful to him. It says that no matter how badly our mother treats us at least one parent loves us.

    Christmas is a very special time for us. Daddy doesn't have money to buy us expensive toys but he does his best to make us happy. Mother knows how to sew and she makes most of our clothes. Without exception each one of us has a new dress for Christmas morning. It becomes a tradition for the family; as the sun rises, and everything comes to life, we are awakened to strains of music. Daddy loves music and plays his harmonica or the keyboard incessantly. After an early breakfast, all of us get dressed and off we go to the Christmas Market. It's held on the streets of Kingston, where hundreds of sellers display their festive wears for the passers-by, and the smell of fruit cakes, baked ham, sorrel, potato and plum puddings wafts through the air and tickle our nostrils. We revel in the sights and sounds. But our real purpose for being here is for each child to choose a toy. Dolls, fire engines, trucks, doll houses, blown up plastic Santas, reindeers, elves, all manner of objects are on display. We return home with the object of choice.

We love our Daddy. He is the stabilizing force in our lives, but he's no match for his wife. He does his best to provide for the family and protect his children, but he can't escape her wrath.

"Blessed be the God and father of our Lord Jesus Christ who hath blessed us with all spiritual blessings in heavenly places in Christ Jesus
According as he hath chosen us in him before the foundation of the world, that we should be holy and without blame before him in love.
Having predestinated us unto the adoption of children by Jesus Christ to himself, according to the good pleasure of his will."
Ephesians 1: 3-5 (KJV)

***Life question***: *It is not uncommon for differences to exist between a mother and her child, especially a daughter. What is disquieting is the unrelenting, unbiased hatred mother harbored for all eleven of her children. What horrible event could have occurred in her life to make her so bitter and resentful towards us? Even at this stage of her life she remains estranged from all of us. She has spent time in all our homes, but remains as hateful as ever; no one wants to keep her around. Is this behavior normal, or is it the result of some deep-seated psychological disorder for which help should be sought?*

***Answer:***

## *Chapter Six*

## SOLD FOR A FISTFUL OF DOLLARS

My mother's friend owns a beautiful home on the hill in one of St. Andrew's elite neighborhoods. His position in the country's government is extolled along with how good he has been to the family. I'm introduced to him and told that he is my godfather, and should be called Uncle Duke. We begin making regular visits to his other plush home in another well-heeled neighborhood. The servants cater to us especially after I'm introduced as:

"Miss Marcia, Uncle Duke's goddaughter".

I love visiting the kitchen; there I can have whatever I wish from the refrigerator. We get to take car rides in big cars driven by men who open the doors for us. We feel rich and important. We feel good when Uncle Duke takes us on his lap, asks us about school and reminds us to do well so we can achieve success in the future. Then he gives us twenty-dollar bills from his wallet, telling us to buy ourselves something special from him. Uncle Duke is a very important man, one of the leaders of the Island, a Minister in the government. When he appears on television making long speeches or having a debate with other ministers, we sit with open mouths watching in awe as he and the others made all types of rules and regulations for the Island. To be known and be related to him is great. We tell all our peers who he is, feeling special when they treat us with more respect because we are related to the Honorable M.H. Newell, Minister of Government. Often, while visiting the home in Englewood, our mother takes us out into the front yard telling us to look up to the hills ahead of us. Magnificent homes rise up out of the blasted rocks and there nestled among the foliage is the one we are trying to get a glimpse of.

# The Odyssey of Survival

"Do you see it? The yellow one, that's the ministerial home of your godfather." This sounds important, but it's lost on me.

One Sunday morning a few months after my twelfth birthday, my mother tells me to take a bath and get dressed because we are going out. She lays out my best Sabbath dress for me to wear. This must be important. Church clothes are never worn to anyplace, except church. For the first time in my life Mother straightens my hair. I feel like a grown up. All dressed up with long smooth pressed hair falling down my back.

"Where are you going?" My sisters ask.

"I don't know Mama just told me to get dressed."

They admired my new hairdo and wondering out loud when theirs will be straightened also. Although it's Sunday, Daddy had gone to work to earn overtime pay. In silence my Mother and I travel to a mysterious place. We board three buses; the last one takes us up on a hill. "Where are we going?" I wonder, but know better than to ask. I follow directions; do as I am told and go where I'm sent. Our upbringing taught us to be seen but not heard. I ask no questions. Like a lamb, I'm silently led to the slaughter.

We exit the bus and walk a short distance up a private road past a few beautiful homes then enter through the gate of one of them. Mother speaks to me for the first time since leaving home.

"This is your godfather's ministerial home, the one we tried showing to you from his Avondale home. He has been good to the family and I want you to do whatever he tells you to. Do you hear me?"
"Yes mama." I can't possibly think of what I would be told to do. I am excited to be in such a grand place as a Ministerial home.

The minister himself warmly greets us. He kisses my mother on the cheek and compliments me on how nicely I have grown and how pretty I am. He ushers us to the verandah where he serves us cool drinks and cake explaining that all the help has gone home for the weekend. He and Mother chat while I tentatively explore the place. I lightly touch the piano keys; run my hand over the soft chairs and looking at the beautiful pictures on the walls. I soak up the newness of it all, trying to remember everything so I can tell my sisters every detail. There is a peculiar smell, not unpleasant, just strange. I sniff the air trying to make a connection with something. I can't do it. About an hour into the visit I hear Mother calling me. I answer and come running from the back verandah which I was exploring. She tells me to go to my godfather. He gets up from the chair and tells me to follow him, because he has something to show to me. I follow him up three steps, which lead onto the second floor where the bedrooms are located. He opens the first door on the left telling me to go in. I obey. It's a large bedroom with its own bathroom. He offers me a seat on the edge of the bed and I sit down. He questions me about school.

"How are you doing in school? Are you getting good grades? What's your favorite subject? Are you being a good girl?"

I answer all his questions. He then begins running his hand over my newly pressed hair, telling me how pretty I am and how nice my hair looks. I thank him. His hand travels to my knee and begins a journey to where? – I don't want to know. I shift my body, moving my legs away from him. He roughly pulls them back, telling me to be a good girl. I know that this is wrong; he should not be touching my legs attempting to get his hands under my skirt. I pull my skirt down further, adjusting my body further away from him. He yanks up my skirt and tries sticking his hand between my legs. Tears are running down my face. I jump up from the bed running for the door.

"No, please let me go back outside to Mama."

He grabs my arm shoving me back down on the bed. I'm crying loudly.

"What are you doing?" I asked, he ignores my question trying to get on top of me. "Stop it. Uncle Duke, please stop it."

Cursing under his breath, he opens the door; I immediately jump off the bed thinking he is allowing me to go free. Instead, he sticks his head out the door and calls my mother. I'm standing directly behind him crying. Surely she will rescue me from this wretched man. Mother treads the stairs to the room. He steps halfway out the door to speak to her.

"Talk to her. She is not cooperating."

My mother walks into the room. I look up at her expectantly. She slaps my face, yelling.

"What is the matter with you? Didn't I tell you to do as you are told? Get back in that room and don't make me have to come back up here or you will be sorry."

Turning on her heels, she waltzes out of the room. He comes back in, and this time he locks the door behind him pocketing the key.

"Get on the bed." He orders.

I stand my ground; crying. He grabs my arm, viciously pulling me towards the bed, pushing me down on it. With all my strength I fight, but could not fight off the advances of a sixty-two year old man; who has the permission of my mother to rape me. He's trying to yank off my panties and I'm fighting to keep my legs tightly crossed. I sob loudly from deep within. He pushes my legs apart, letting go of my right leg. I immediately draw it up to my chest. He grabs my heel pulling it back down. He uses his right knee to keep my legs down and apart. He now has me pinned down on the bed, my panties have been thrown someplace and my legs are apart. I'm crying. He uses his right hand to guide himself as he plunges his manhood into my twelve year old virgin body. I scream as the air rushed out of my lungs. He firmly clasps his hand over my mouth. I bite his hand, but that has no effect on him. He is bent on raping me and I'm powerless to stop him.

Only the fire of hell could be this painful. Every part of my body feels as if it's being consumed from within. I begin choking while thrashing my legs around to get him off and out of my body. I beat against his chest twisting my head from side to side trying to free his hand. But all my efforts are in vain. Effortlessly he holds me in a tight grip. My heart is so full of fear and hate that I think I'm about to explode. "Somebody help me. O God help me. Why is this happening to me? Why did my mother bring me here for this to happen? God where are you? Please rescue me out of this."

"You are a feisty little one, aren't you." he mutters, as he violently and viciously rapes me.

When he's through ravishing my body, he slowly removes his hand from my mouth, telling me to be quiet. By then I'm in too much pain to be anything but quiet. He swings off the bed going to his bathroom where he cleans himself. A few minutes later he emerges with a wet washcloth. The sheets had been pulled up to my neck trying to hide myself from him. He yanks the sheet from my hands, pushes my legs apart and uses the washcloth to clean the blood and his fluid off of me. Turning my head away from him, I allow the tears to run down my cheeks soaking the pillow and settling in a pool under my head.

"Stay where you are for a little while, then get dressed and come join us."

He picks up his pants and underwear off the floor laying them on a chair, and sits down on the bed next to my head. I turn my head to the other side as I lay there in agony, my body is throbbing and I'm unable to move. My insides feel as if it had been churned in a blender. He's stroking my legs. I pull them away from his hand.

"You need to learn to be obedient and then you won't get hurt. Your mother and I have big plans for you. You will be groomed to be a part of all this one-day, but you must be obedient. Keep your mouth shut about this and anything else that happens within these walls.

# The Odyssey of Survival

Do you understand me?"

Unable to speak I nodded in the affirmative. He lights and smokes a cigarette, then he takes a drink from a glass, setting the glass down, he gets on the bed and lying down beside me. I turn away onto my side, quietly sobbing.

"This is the type of behavior I am talking about." he said, as he roughly grabs my shoulders, forcing me onto my back. To my horror he gets himself over me, enters my body and begins raping me again. I am in the belly of hell with the worst creature on earth. I'm transfixed on the pain. This cannot be happening. It must be a very bad nightmare from which I will wake up. But it was not a dream and I am awake.

Like a lioness I fight, tearing at his hair, biting his shoulders, beating on his back. He doesn't even flinch from the blows. Again I lose the fight. I beg God to take my life because the pain is too much for me to endure. How can this be happening to me? From somewhere deep within the recesses of my soul survival kicks in. My mind removes itself from what's happening to me. My body is being raped but my mind takes flight elsewhere to a safer place. I'm singing. "Jesus loves the little children all the children of the world, red and yellow black and white they are precious in his sight, Jesus loves the little children of the world."

Why doesn't my mother help me? Does she know what's going on in the bedroom? Of course she knows. My 'loving' mother had dressed me up, pressed my hair, and taken me on a mysterious trip to a big, beautiful ministerial home. She presented me to a powerful minister within the government of the country, my godfather. She seated herself in a comfortable chair sipping a cool drink eating delicious cake, enjoying the ambiance of her surroundings, while I am being raped a few feet away. As I ponder this I realize that this was not an accident; it had been planned between my mother and my godfather. I have become a victim of my mother's evil scheming. My mind cannot process the enormity of the situation at this time. The only thing I know is that an evil, worse than death have touched me in the worst way. Something worst than death has crawled into my soul taking up residence within my very existence, and my mother is in agreement with it.

He satisfies himself, he cleans himself, he gets dressed. He tells me to get dressed and rejoin them on the verandah. He walks out of the room as if nothing had happened. Through the open window I hear him join my mother on the verandah. They engage in conversation and laughter. Gingerly I get off the bed, testing the level of pain that shoots through me. I hunch over for a couple minutes, and then drag myself into the bathroom. Looking down at myself, the sight of blood and my red swollen vulva shocks me. The pain is excruciating. I clean myself, wincing at every touch. Pulling my underwear up, the touch of the nylon against my skin is unbelievably painful. I leave them hanging down as far as I can.

Bawling gut-wrenching agony, I continue getting dressed. Staggering to lean against the bathroom door. I don't know what to do. How am I going to face my mother? I feel dirty and ashamed. What am I going to do? Trying to regain my composure I wash my face, comb my hair, straighten my dress and waddle out of the room. I go into the kitchen and pour myself a glass of water. Then as carefully as I can, I sit down on the edge of a chair in the living room. I'm expecting my mother to come see how I was, but she never came. She cast not one glance in my direction.

Almost an hour later, my mother decided it was time to go. She calls my name. I answer but don't move. They prepare to separate, entering the room. I stand up. Standing there with my head hung down low and my legs apart, I wish the ground could open up and swallow me. Right there before my eyes, my godfather takes his wallet from his back pocket removes a few hundred-dollar bills and paid my mother for the service I had rendered. At that moment I realized that,
 "I had been sold. I was sold by my mother for a fistful of dollars."

"And he said unto me. My grace is sufficient for thee. For my strength is made perfect in weakness.
Most gladly therefore will I rather glory in my *infirmities, that the power of Christ may rest upon me.*
Therefore I take pleasures in infirmities, in reproaches, in necessities, in persecutions, in distresses for Christ's sake. For when I am weak, then am I strong."
2 Corinthians 12:9 10

***Life question:*** *It is inconceivable that a mother would expose her children to this type of evil. The scars have never healed. They have remained as open wounds, raw and painful today as the day they were inflicted forty years ago. Should the accomplice in a crime such as this be charged even if the perpetrator is deceased? Should my mother be held responsible for contributing to the delinquency of minors?*

***Answer:***

## Chapter Seven

## BETRAYALS

Thoughts swirl around in my mind. What should I do? Should I tell her about what had happened? Should I ask her why she had taken me up there? Should I tell her how much he had hurt me? Did she have previous knowledge of his intentions? Was she a part of his plan? Walking is difficult. The throbbing and pain between my legs up into my stomach is still very intense, causing me to lag behind, unable to keep up with her long strides. After walking for a few minutes to the bus stop I decide to say something.

"Mama." I mutter. That is the only word, which escapes my lips.
"Shut up." She answers glaring at me. "I don't want to hear anything from you."

I close my mouth and keep it closed. I know that the events will never be spoken about. The shame and pain is swelling up in me, it's getting more intense even as we walk silently along. I begin feeling like a pressure cooker. I hope I don't explode.

My sisters are waiting for us to return home. When we walk in the door they wait for mother to leave the room and begin asking. "Where did you go? What happened? Why do you look so sad, didn't you have fun? Forcing a smile I promise to give details later. Following in my sisters, Amelia and Victoria's footsteps, fourteen years earlier, I say nothing. Locking myself in the bathroom, I furiously fan between my legs. Gently I press a cold wet washcloth to the swollen area; I do everything conceivable to stop the pain. Nothing works.

# The Odyssey of Survival

Again I dry my tears, straighten my clothing and go to bed, remaining there for the remainder of the evening. This is only the first of many trips I make; accompanied by my mother to the man on the hill. It becomes almost a ritual. She presses my hair, orders me to get dressed, and we travel to the home. I sit in the living room quietly crying. When he is ready he grabs my arm taking me to his bedroom. There I'm raped. He doesn't call my mother to slap my face anymore. He does the beatings. He pulls me up on my knees pushing my face down into the pillows. When he enters me from behind, I scream bloody murder. He punches me in my back, slapping my buttocks. He turns me onto my back and slaps my face several times. My mouth begins bleeding. He tells me to shut up if I didn't want to get hurt. I learn to remain still, it's useless fighting, I never win. My mind finds refuge someplace else. I become disconnected from the pain in my body. Mother waits for him to return from raping me, then I hear them laughing and talking. After a while longer, she gets paid, and we make the silent trip home. I don't know what happens with my siblings except they are put through the same rituals of getting their hair pressed, dressed in Sabbath finery and taken out on a Sunday afternoon. Whatever happened remains with them. Cheryl, the youngest is eight years my junior. I don't know when Mother sacrificed her. She is barely twelve years old when she is taken up to Uncle Duke's house. Mother takes her to the bedroom leaving her there at his mercy. He begins touching her. She begins to cry. She recounts being so ashamed, and conscious of her torn underwear that she stands there immobilized, offering no resistance to his probing hands. She is out of daughters to be sold. I wonder what she will do now.

Just when I thought I had heard it all, another shocking disclosure takes my breath away. Victoria had given birth to two boys before migrating to Canada. To my amazement she tells me during a telephone conversation that Uncle Duke is the father of her eldest son. She had also been one of his victims. He had not only repeatedly raped her, but had gotten her pregnant.

"Oh my goodness, does Mama know that Uncle Duke is

# The Odyssey of Survival

Miguel's father?"

"Of course she knows. She is the one who took me to his house and waited outside while he raped me. When I found out I was pregnant I told her it happened when she took me up there. She slapped me in my face threatening to have me killed if I dared to say such a thing again."

Mother tells Uncle Duke that Victoria's baby doesn't belong to him, and he in turn refuses to provide support for the child. Victoria decides to fight back. She had been unable to fight for herself, now she will fight for her child's welfare. She gathers all her strength and marches down to the courthouse. There she files a suit against the Minister in the Island's court for child support. Uncle Duke gets served with the court papers and throws a royal fit. He barks orders at the chauffer to go pick up Mrs. Macaroon and bring her to him. She arrives at the home and he screams bloody murder at her. She is infuriated. Victoria defies the threats of Mother and the minister, determined to carry out her plan of forced child support. She was sixteen years old when she became pregnant.

While standing in a group of other mothers seeking support for their children waiting for her case to be heard, a stranger speaks into her ear. "You better get out of here while you still can. If you ever open your mouth in here today it will be the last time you open your mouth, and you will be dead as soon as you walk out of the door."

Spinning around, on her heels, she finds no one. The speaker has easily disappeared into the mass of people waiting around. In fear she hastily leaves the courtroom, never again trying to get the support she and her son is entitled to. The irony of the situation was that, mother, who, for years has been trading Victoria off to this man for money, had the gall to tell him that the child was not his, and therefore should not be supported by him. Like the coward he is, knowing he has been raping her for years, he chose to believe his partner in crime.

With mother's consent, since Victoria was fourteen years old she has been spending nights with him at his home and in hotels. One night he has the immense pleasure of having both Victoria and Lynnette (the younger sister) in bed with him at the same time. Going from one to the other, fulfilling his most sadistic desire with two very young; very unwilling girls. They have no choice. That has been taken away by their mother. Victoria recalls how during the night, after he was finished with her, she was looking for a way to clean herself, she finds his hanky on the nightstand, and uses it as a washrag. In the morning he reaches for his hanky, instead of finding it well pressed, he found a wet sticky white rag. He is furious, cursing at her for her stupidity. Since mother is not present to collect her fee for the use of her daughters, the bounty was sent home in a sealed envelope with the victims. We are under duress; all I have ever wanted is the love of my mother. More than life itself, I desire the open arms of my mother. I will give my right arm if she asks for it as payment for her love. I will do anything to make her love me. We feel like aliens in a world where mothers love their children, and children adore and revere their mothers. We have spent years trying to figure out what we have done wrong, causing us to be devoid of so precious an affection. As children we felt inadequate. To compensate for the absence of her love we pour our emotions into our father and one another. As desperately as we need our mother's love, we love one another. Along with the pact we make with each other not to allow her to kill any one of us, we also promise never to treat our children the way she has treated us. We decide to do the exact opposite of everything she has done. None of us wishes to be like her. We are afraid of inheriting any trace of her disposition, and quickly squash anything noticeable in our behavior with the slightest reminder of her. When someone comments on the similarities of my features to my mother's, it is quickly denied.

"No, I look like my father."

I laugh at a joke, and someone commented that I sound like my mother. Instantly I set to work changing the pitch and range of my voice. We want to be nothing like her, bearing no resembling traits or traces of the woman who brought us into the world. We realize that for us to survive we have to do more than make a pact with one another. We must find ways to cope with our inner emotional turmoil. I begin burying myself in fantasy books. I keep them hidden in my textbooks pretending to study, instead devouring great flights and fairytales.

Janice finds solace in writing poetry. Her book of poetry, called "Bareface Pickney" has earned her the recognition she deserves. An example of one of her poems as she tries to find answers to the questions asked by all of us follows:

'A CHILD'S WISH'
By Alicia Janice Macaroon

A very hard thing for me to do
Is to write a poem in praise of you
For though I try, we all know
That love and tenderness you do not show

I would love to tell my friends
How your children you always defend
How you rocked us on your knees
In love with you we'd always be

I dream of telling everyone
That you will always understand
That individual we'll forever be
That you accepted "radical me"

That you loved us no matter what
You thanked God for whatever you got
You nurtured us with love and care
We always knew that you were near

# The Odyssey of Survival

I hope and pray that I could say
You showed us tenderness everyday
You guided us with the facts of life
You never threatened with a knife

You gave us positive views of you
The wonderful things you always do
You hugged and kissed us in formative days
You talked us out of childhood fears

But sad to say I cannot lie
My childhood days will make me cry
I cannot write the traditional lines
Caregivers come in many kinds

So though I desperately want to say
I love you more with each passing day
I have to hold my pen awhile
For there is bitterness though a child

So please try now to make amends
We do so want to be your friend
Your children want to take care of you
To turn the clock and start anew
For our days on earth could be few.

"The Lord is my shepherd; I shall not want.  He makes me to lie down in green pastures; he leads me beside the still waters.
He restores my soul; he leads me in the paths of righteousness for his namesake.
Yea, though I walk through the valley of the shadow of death, I will fear no evil; for thou art with me; thy rod and thy staff they comfort me.
Thou prepares a table before me in the presence of mine enemies, thou anointed my head with oil; my cup runs over.
Surely goodness and mercy shall follow me all the days of my life, and I will dwell in the house of the Lord for ever."
Psalm 23

# The Odyssey of Survival

***Life question****: Is it reasonable to deduce that the experiences of our childhood shape our future behavior, dictating who we are and what we become? When young children become victims of insidious crimes are we held, even partially responsible, for the actions of the adults committing the crimes? Should we have disregarded the threats of our mother, risked our lives, and reported what had been happening to us by one of the country's leaders? Would anyone have believed us, if they had chosen to deny the allegations? Remember, our mother would have taken his side against us. By bringing it out in the open, could we have spared the younger ones the ordeal? But to whom could we have gone? Would anyone have believed us? Who could we tell that the Minister was really a rapist, and more so, that our mother had sold her soul and her daughters to him? What could we have done? What would you have done?*

***Answer:***

## Chapter Eight

## GOOD AND EVIL; TRUTH AND LIES

The highly renowned Rev J.C. Palmer evangelist for the Seventh Day Adventist Conference will be arriving in Kingston to conduct a four-week crusade under the big tent at Marverly Park. Excitement fills the air as the news is voiced throughout the church community. The impending arrival of the preacher caused a stir in the hearts of the religious, and awe in the eyes of the teenagers. The flyers proclaim.

"Get ready to be blessed for the mighty man of God is coming to town and lives will be changed. Prepare to attend nightly meetings under the big tent."

We have never attended evangelistic crusades, especially ones held under a tent. Excitingly we await the commencement of these meetings. Rev. Palmer does not disappoint his audience. He has the crowd the first night. Skillfully he teaches the people about God's love for them, about His forgiveness and plan of salvation for each one of us. He tells us how Christ came to earth to save us from our sins and our past sins will be forgiven if we repent. To complement his teachings he brought in some of the best musicians and singers to minister to us. We are transfixed by the encouraging words of salvation and accompanying music. My family attends the meetings as often as possible. Patricia and I are allowed to attend the meetings by ourselves on weeknights. Our parents are too tired and the others are considered too young. After meetings conclude at night a couple of the young men walk us home, being careful to retreat just before turning that last corner where they would be observed by our mother, who is religiously sitting upon her bed hidden behind the curtains watching through the window to see if we dare have anyone walk into her line of vision. Carefully we protect our companions, enjoying the unexpected freedom of being out of the house at least three nights weekly. The teachings caused a stirring in my heart and a deep longing to experience the everlasting and unconditional love of God. My life has been so debased and void of love that the prospect of a God loving me enough to have died for me seemed surreal. I crave to be loved in that fashion. Although we have been attending church for years, this is the first time we became exposed to the nature of God. The Reverend's words have a great impact on both of us. We want to hear more about this God who loves us so much He had given up his life, had died on a cross to save us into his kingdom, so we could live with him for Eternity. We certainly needed someone to love us and God sounded like he was the only one who could do so. Patricia and I along with many others decide to give our lives to God. When the appeal was made for those who wanted to be baptized we are among the first ones who respond to the call. The response to the appeal is so great that the leaders decide that the baptism would have to be held at a beach for the facilities at the tent could not accommodate the volume of new believers. A trip to the beach was always a treat regardless of the occasion. One week later on a beautiful Sunday morning three chartered buses filled with sinners seeking freedom and forgiveness of our sins are loaded up and head for the Gunboat Beach. We sing the songs of redemption and praise as the buses roll along filled with people, happy in our newfound Lord. The mass baptism of about three hundred is a great success. No one drowns, and we all rejoice, singing even louder on the return trip. The crusade ends with hundreds of new converts being added to the church. The existing congregations in the surrounding areas gladly accept some of the new members, but there is still an overflow with no church of our own to attend. The conference of the denomination hears about this problem and sends a representative to assess the needs of the people. They give permission for a new church to be built. The property is acquired and plans for a suitable house of worship begins.

Daddy, the carpenter, along with most of the other men volunteers to build the church. Sundays and every evening after work this dedicated band of men hammers, pounds, saws and nails. In no time at all the beginnings of a structure appear out of the ground. Up it goes, taking shape, until on a memorable Sabbath morning the newly formed congregation has the immense pleasure of worshipping in our very own church. My family is proud to be among the founding members of this brand new church. It was not much of a church at this stage. The men have erected four walls and cut openings for windows, but no windows have yet been installed. When the wind blows up the dust we all get dusty: when it rains everyone gathers in the middle of the sanctuary to avoid getting wet. The seats are long slabs of planks nailed down on stumps with no supporting backs, the floor is dirt and the roof is zinc, which leaks at the places where they are joined. But we love our little church. The sweat of its congregation had built it. It belongs to us. The congregation grows until we are appointed a leader. Pastor Woodburn a kind grandfatherly man becomes our shepherd. He leads his little band of sheep very well, and we love him.

Across the street from our church is another church, which belongs to a strange religious sect. While we worship quietly and piously with serene bowed heads, this church is loud and noisy. On Sunday nights both churches hold services but we have a difficult time hearing our speakers as their shouts of praise drowns out everything else. This type of worship fascinates us. Ignoring the orders of our leaders and parents not to enter the premises, we creep silently across the street to watch firsthand the happenings in this church. We watch with wide-eyed amazement as they jump and prance around, the women having to be wrapped in sheets to prevent total exposure of themselves to all onlookers, and the men falling on the ground shouting, while the children seem delirious with whatever possesses them. We can't get enough of these performances and attend Sunday night services mainly to watch these people. The trouble we get into when the adults of our congregation discover us peering through the door and windows at "the crazy people" doesn't stop us; we are fascinated by this type of worship. Who are they worshipping? Is it the same God who we ever so quietly and piously worship? And to whom is he listening. Can he hear them better because they shout so loudly, and is he able to hear us over the din of their noise? The new congregation needs everyone to participate in the services of the church. We jump into action becoming involved in many areas.

# The Odyssey of Survival

I teach children's Sabbath School, and become the secretary of youth services called Adventist Youth, (AY).

Our parents, who both sing very well, become choir members. (Mother sings soprano and daddy has a beautiful bass voice) I don't know what happened to my voice. I am tone deaf. Another good thing comes out of the new congregation. I find a friend. I am fourteen years old, and somehow we are drawn to each other. I admire this tall young girl who is three years my senior. Kathy and I became close. Her parents join the church in its early days. She has a younger sister who is Bridget's age and they also form a friendship. This is good. We become a foursome. We whisper to each other on Sabbaths and realize that we are both being abused by our mothers. Kathy lives with her mother and stepfather and is disliked by her mother. Although we compared notes on their treatment of us I am very careful never to mention the sexual abuse which my mother has been exposing us to. The shame of it makes me feel almost responsible and I am very afraid of anyone discovering what has been happening to me.

Kathy is allowed to visit our home on Sabbath afternoons and sometimes I have the rare treat of visiting her home. Their home is huge and has fruit trees in the backyard. Their mangos grow in abundance. I always leave her home with a bag of mangos, to everyone's delight. I'm being beaten in Kathy's presence. The simple infraction of contradicting my mother on a point resulted in being kicked to the ground and pounded upon, until my blood spewed. It's a Sabbath afternoon; mother had pealed her lungs out on the choir earlier, shouting Amen to the sermon on love and forgiveness. She slaps and spits in my face. A punch to the stomach folds me over in pain. As I bend over from the impact she punches me in the back. I remember hearing Kathy begging her to stop.

"Sis. Mac, are you going to kill her?" she asks.

Ranting and screaming that I think I'm a big woman, she kicks me, as I fall to the ground she stomps in my sides. Kathy tries pulling her off of me, but she is roughly pushed away. When my mother has

## The Odyssey of Survival

satisfied herself she administers one last kick, then walks away, eaving me a bloody mess, with a threat to kill me later. My friend kneels at my side trying to comfort me. She helps me up to my feet and to the bathroom to clean my face. My tears mingle with blood and stream down my face. I lean on my friend's shoulder, whimpering how much I hate my mother. She comforts me, dries my tears, and stems the blood flow. I compose myself and we try to hide the bruises as best we could before leaving home to attend AY at church. Slowly we walk along the road, trying desperately to hide my distressed, pathetic state from passers-by. We enjoy attending church meetings, and find it easier to endure the hardships of the week, because Sabbath is coming. There we find a little freedom and are reminded that no matter how bad things are, we shouldn't give up because God loves and cares about us. At times I find it difficult to believe that God really cares about me. The question of why is He allowing such awful things to happen to us is always on my lips. I constantly question God in prayer. But there is no response. I still find some comfort in the words of the pastor, and it's these words of encouragement, which keep me going more than anything else. I keep praying and hoping that God will do something to make my life better. I don't know what to expect, but I'm convinced He will hear and help me. I just hope it's soon, before mother kills me.

Time drags on and my life becomes worse from abuse and misuse. Enduring the evil of my godfather and the wretched hate of my mother, I begin to lose hope and faith in God. He had seemed so real and so close to me. During those meetings under the tent, I felt as if he held me in his arms. When I was baptized at the Gunboat beach, I felt as if I was in His very presence. When I worship at church with the other believers my heart soars heavenward. What I can't understand is why has He turned his back on me? What have I done to make him hide his face from me allowing these two people to commit such evils against me? Over time I become so disenchanted with life that I think God must have given up on me. So I give up on him. I go to church because I'm forced to, but my heart has become hard and dead. I don't want to and refuse to have anything to do with the God of my mother. I no longer feel like one of God's children. My life is on a

## The Odyssey of Survival

slippery slope to hell with nothing to stop my headlong descent. I keep attending church, but my heart has become a solid rock.

    The years following my baptism are terrible. I had hoped that by becoming a baptized member of God's church my mother would stop selling me to my godfather. But my hopes have been dashed. I had hoped that she would now reconsider and change her actions as she witnessed our participation in church activities, but she is bent on continuing what she had started. The day of my first rape was the beginning of many years of rapes and abuse by the same person. With more frequency than I can or care to record my mother ordered me to get myself ready, and the now familiar trip to the ministerial home on the hill is made. There is no use protesting, I will only be abused twice, first by her beating and later being raped by my godfather.

    The chauffeured car frequently pulls up at the gate, the chauffeur gets out, a letter is handed to my mother, and I would be ordered to take a bath, get dressed and present myself where I have been ordered to appear. At times I'll be there for two days at a time, missing school, if he desired my presence during the week. Upon my return Daddy would question me as to my whereabouts. I'm told to simply tell him that I was at Uncle Duke's. I long to confide in him, to tell him what's really going on, but I fear for my life too much. Bridget and I accompany him to St. Thomas, it's one of the rare occasions when he drives himself. Returning to Kingston we are sitting in the back seat amusing ourselves. He looks at us through the rear view mirror and orders me to climb over and get into the seat next to him. Bridget and I look at each other, but neither one moves. He barks his order a second time, but we remain seated. He pulls the car over onto the shoulder of the road and gets out. He yanks the door open dragging me out of the back seat, shoving me into the front seat. He climbs back in cursing me for my disobedience while he tries using his fingers inside of me to pleasure himself. Sitting stiffly in the seat and keeping my legs tightly closed I fight him, refusing to allow him entry. He removed his hand in disgust and orders me to get back in the rear of the car. At the end of the journey we are unceremoniously dropped off at home.

# The Odyssey of Survival

I am fifteen years old and about to be graduating from high school, my mother takes me to him. He has his way with me and she receives a handsome reward. I want to go to college. My lifetime dream is to attend college, then law school to become a lawyer. Before graduation, when students are being prepared to take "O" and "A" level exams, hoping to secure enough subjects to be considered likely applicants for acceptance into college I'm told not to even bother thinking about that, because I was going to be sent to a business school to learn business management skills so I could be an assistant to my godfather in his political career. My ambitions are high, but they have been dashed. I have no way to pay for the classes, no way to support myself in college, so my dream becomes just that – a dream, another bad dream. My entire life has been a bad dream, mostly a nightmare out of which I have been struggling to awaken. But somehow the fog of evil looms so large and hangs so low over me, that I can't seem to shake off the destructive hand that I have been dealt. I have not been able to achieve the level of success for which I have worked so hard and for so long. My mother constantly berates us, always telling us that we will never achieve anything in life, we'll never amount to much and we'll never be successful. On many, many occasions, when she gets particularly mad at her bunch of unwanted children, she removes her breasts from within her clothing, beat on them with her fist, place a burning match too close for comfort to her nipples, call upon God's name, then inform us that we are cursed forever, because we have caused our mother to "burn her breast for us". Am I cursed forever? Has God cursed all of us?

Church, ahh Church. During all the years of my mother selling her children, compounded by her desire and attempts to kill us, she has never missed one Sabbath from church. She remains a fervent church attendee and all of us, regardless of the "murderation" (a word coined by Janice to describe mother's intent) endured a few hours earlier, we are required to wash our faces, dry our eyes, get dressed, and go to church. Not one of nine daughters has the privilege of giving their most precious irreplaceable gift given to them by God to their husband. Not one of us is able to be innocent virgins on our wedding night. She has taken it away from all of us. Not one of us have had

# The Odyssey of Survival

their dreams, the dream of every little girl of walking out of her mother's house in the most beautiful white wedding dress, to meet her husband at the alter, with the blessing of her mother. None of her eleven children knows what it feels like to be hugged by their mother and told. "I love you." Not one has ever had the opportunity of sitting on Mother's knees, telling her about a problem, asking for her advice, and listening to her wisdom. Not one of us has had the privilege of experiencing a mother's limitless love, that love that causes mothers to rise to the defense of their children, that love that makes a mother furious at the very indication that someone would entertain the thought of hurting one of her children, that love that even if the child did wrong will make you go to battle to protect your own flesh and blood, that love that makes a mother say "you'll be better off if you hurt me instead of my child, because if you hurt my child I will kill you."

The opposite is true; our mother creates situations which endanger our lives, making us easy targets for the actions of unscrupulous men. She spends her life trying to kill us herself, creating for us an unstable, abusive, dysfunctional environment. We have not learned how to love, how to trust, how to accept love from others. Like chickens we have spent our lives scratching around in the ground, looking for a place to lie down and find rest. It has eluded us. We remain a sad bunch of unloved, unwanted children, still grappling and finding no answer to the question.

Why does our mother hate us?

Both parents are very active in church, mother more so. She teaches a Sabbath school class, sings on the choir, and is a deaconess. The truth is that Sabbath is the only happy day in our lives. It's the only day that we can escape her wrath for a few hours, but God help you if you committed an infraction during this holy day; your skin will be peeled after the sacred hours are over. Even with this always hanging over our heads we still enjoy Sabbath. It's also the only day that strangers are allowed to come over. We could bring home a friend or two and every week a couple of adults accompanied us home to partake of Sabbath lunch. No one on entering our home can ever imagine how badly we are treated. Having people around brings out the best in us, so that our behavior is impeccable. We smile, serve the guests, enjoy the meal, and pretend that we live normal lives. Thank God, regardless of how a child is treated, that child will grow into a teenager and ultimately into adulthood. By His grace we grow and a small ray of hope flickers in our hearts. We begin maturing and slowly we feel that if we have made it this far, we just might make it after all. We trudge through our days, trying to keep out of mother's way, struggling to maintain our sanities, keeping quiet about our situation at home. Maybe, just maybe, we might survive mother.

Patricia suffers terribly at her hands. I do not know for sure if Uncle Duke also raped her, but I do know that she is as hated as the rest of us. One day, Patricia did or said something wrong. After beating her to a frazzle, mother douses her with kerosene oil, lighting a match to set her on fire. Patricia screams from the burning pain of the kerosene and must have seen death approach as her mother strikes the match with every intention of killing her. Lester, our brother, happened to be visiting that day, and it is his swift intervention that saves Patricia. Grabbing mother's arm, he wrestles the match from her. The rest of us huddle together watching in horror the near demise of our sister. I get in trouble a lot with Patricia. We constantly irk each other. She's two years my senior, so for two years we're in high school together. One day on our way home from school in the company of a couple other students, one of them asks why our features are so different and why we had different surnames but are sisters. I responded.

"Oh, she is not my sister, but since she lives with us, my mother allows her to attend school with us."

The moment the words are out of my mouth I know that I had dug my own grave. Patricia is furious as our schoolmates laugh. What I'd said will become new gossip around school tomorrow.

Storm clouds brew in her face, and she hauls darts of hate at me from her eyes. She threatens to "fix my business" as soon as we get

# The Odyssey of Survival

home. She certainly fixed my business as she beat-up on me, and death almost became my new best friend when she tells mother. I am beaten close to an early grave. I deserve this beating. It was a cruel thing to say, and I take this opportunity to publicly apologize to her.

"Patricia I am sorry for hurting your feelings with this and other hurtful comments I have made. Please forgive me."

Somehow Patricia is able to communicate the abuses against her to our older sisters in Canada. Amelia and Victoria begin the process of sponsoring her into Canada. She will finally get to leave mother's house. As departure day draws closer, she lives on pins and needles, as our mother constantly threatens not to allow her to leave the country if she does or says anything to her displeasure. The rest of us wonder.

"When will we be able to escape? Will the day ever come when one of the sisters will sponsor us into Canada?"

Patricia is seventeen years old. She tries desperately to hide her enthusiasm. We are happy for her, and will miss her, but we're glad to see her getting out of hell. At least one has escaped. Maybe there is hope for us eventually. No one, except Mother is allowed to accompany her to the airport. Tearfully we hug saying goodbyes, not knowing when we will see her again. As the taxi pulls away from the gate we cry, watching it long after it's out of sight. Mother returns from the airport announcing that Patricia was on her way. Other than that she doesn't say a word. At the airport Patricia has a rude awakening. She is known as Patricia Verona Starcky, the last child for my mother's first husband. Mother tells us that she was pregnant with Patricia when her father, Billy Starcky died.

Late arrival at the airport affords them little time to check in. Over the intercom comes an announcement for the last passenger, Patricia Morales, to board right away. They do not react; it doesn't concern them. A few minutes later the message is repeated with a last call warning.

# The Odyssey of Survival

Mother says. "Hurry up that's you they are calling."

"No its not, they are calling Patricia Morales."

"That's you. Here's your passport and ticket. Hurry up before the plane leaves you."

She pushes the documents into her hands. This is the first time Patricia gets a glimpse of her passport and ticket. Mother bids her a hasty good-by, turns around and walks away.

Stunned and confused, but with no time to question mother, Patricia hurries to the gate. Soon Air Canada is taxing down the runway and she is off the shores of Jamaica. Patricia settles in her seat, and the plane begins its ascent taking her to a new land and a new life. Tentatively she opens her passport. What she sees make her gasp in shock. There is a picture of her. That is her correct date and place of birth. But what is that? Under her picture is a strange name. Who is Patricia Verona Morales? Wasn't she Patricia Starcky? If her name is a lie, then who is she? Who is her father? If not Billy Starcky, then who? What is this that has befallen her? How could her mother be this cruel to let her discover this secret in such a manner?

Questions flood her mind. Tears stream down her cheeks. Not only is this the first time she has left home, but also in a treacherous way she discovers that she is not who she and her entire family think she is. What is she going to do? Who is she? Amid her musings and tears the plane arrives at its destination. Each time she is referred to as Miss Morale's tears spring to her eyes, but she mutters thank you and keeps going. Amelia and Victoria are at the airport to welcome her. Shortly after landing she is whisked to Amelia's home where the family welcomes her. Too tired to deal with another emotional upheaval, she decides to get a nights rest before divulging the new information. At breakfast the following morning she tries to explain her discoveries, finding it difficult to do, she passes her passport to Amelia. They ask for an explanation and Patricia recounts what transpired at the airport. Everyone is shocked.

# The Odyssey of Survival

What? How can this be? Why is her name not Starcky? Who is her father?

Patricia has no choice but to assume her new identity. All documents proclaimed her to be Patricia Morales, so Morales she reluctantly becomes. She places a call to mother.

"Hello Mama. How are you?"

"I'm fine. How are you? How was the flight?"

"I'm fine, the flight was alright. I was a little scared when the plane lifted up, and when it landed my ears got all clogged up. The lady next to me gave me a piece of chewing gum, which helped. How is everyone doing?"

"Everyone is ok. Don't waste your sister's money on this call, write a letter."

"Ok Mama, but before you go I need to ask you something. Why does my passport and birth certificate have my name as Morales? Who is my father?"

"Don't ask me any questions. What, because you are now in Canada you think you are a big woman to call me on the telephone and question me?"

"No Mama, but I'm just wondering why you didn't tell me that I had a different father from Amelia and the others. All my life I thought we had the same father who died when you were pregnant with me. If that's not true then who is my father?"

"Gal you want to know who your father is? Well let me tell you. You are the result of one pound of beef. That is your heritage; a pound of beef for some sex. Now don't bother me. Don't ask me any more questions. I owe you no explanations."

# The Odyssey of Survival

Reeling from the exchange Patricia hangs up the telephone, sits down and has a good cry. She must survive this. With Patricia's migration to Canada, I become the eldest child in the home. The responsibilities grow. The preparation of meals for the family becomes mine. Cleaning the house; ironing the clothes (even daddy's underwear has to be ironed); in addition to taking care of the younger children. We are still not allowed to associate with the neighborhood children, so we entertain ourselves in any way we can.

A family of Indian descent moves into the house two doors down from us. The parents fight constantly, until one day the mother packs her bags and left the home, leaving behind five of the most pitiful little children I have ever seen. We are sorry for them. Their father is a drunk who leaves them all day with no food in the house. They stand at the fence looking at us and the other children with wide sad eyes. Their hair is greasy and uncombed and their clothes are filthy. In our mother's absence we share our food with them, handing it over the fence or through the gate. We are careful never to enter their premises, lest our mother hears about our trespassing from a nosey neighbor. We play ball games with them over the fence and try amusing them as much as we can. I possess a good sense of time and am usually able to predict our mothers return from the market.

One fateful day, the little girls look particularly filthy. We can smell their unwashed bodies across two fences. I decide that as soon as mother is safely out of the house I'll call the girls over. I shampoo their hair and sitting on the front steps begin the tedious task of detangling the knots from their hair. Becoming engrossed in our activities, and to our detriment, I lose track of time. Hearing a sound I look up and there is mother coming through the gate. O God. We are dead now.

"What are you doing? What are these filthy children doing over here? Get out of my yard" she screams. "And all of you get inside."

# The Odyssey of Survival

Everyone scatters. We march inside to face the wrath of mother. That is a beating I will never forget. She thumps and slaps and kicks, and stomps on me. Why? All I did was try to help a few needy children. This makes no sense to me. I love and care about children and cannot understand why I'm being punished for lending a helping hand. But then I do not understand much of what my mother does. Where is God? This is a fervent question on our lips and in my heart. Why doesn't He stop her cruelties? Why does he allow her to continue treating us so poorly, while she piously attends church weekly, singing on the choir, teaching Sabbath school and presenting herself as a good person to the world? On several occasions we asked our father why he chose her to be our mother, why couldn't he have chosen a nice person like himself. He tries explaining to us how we would not be the same people if even one of our parents was different. We don't care. We just want a nice mother. We are so tired of her cruelty that we begin hating her. We wish her dead, and at times even talk among ourselves of ways to be rid of her. Somehow, in all of this, we were very aware of the respect that should be shown to her as our mother. No matter what she does, Bridget is always the voice saying to us.

"Stop it she is still your mother." We do not understand. We know that God still expects us to respect her, but we don't have to love her. Do we?

I graduate from business school with an Associates Degree in Business Management and become the personal assistant to the Minister, my godfather and rapist. The same chauffeured car, which, for the past four years frequently picks me up to be molested, now picks me up for work. I work in his office, receive a salary and am driven home at the end of each work day. He has not lost his perverse interest in me but due to the professional environment his advancements become curtailed. I begin to blossom, smiling more, almost like a normal teenager. At church, we enjoy a vibrant youth club called "Pathfinders". The young people reveled in its activities, loving every moment of its grueling drill. "Pathfinders at-ten-tion." Every right foot stomps down, and our arms are held stiffly at our sides. "Pathfinders forward march." Trying our best not to bump into one another. We move forward hopefully swinging the correct arm in unison. Henry, the club's leader takes an interest in my family, but more so in me. He visits the home frequently, and with five club members under the same roof there is plenty to discuss. His special interest in me is flattering and results in a friendship, which blossoms into puppy love. Contact with the opposite sex has been fiercely forbidden. Henry is allowed into our home only because of his position in church. For a few months we whisper into each other's ears on the telephone from the office, all the while being careful not to attract any attention at church.

Much to my surprise he shows up at our home one Sunday afternoon. We pay no special attention to each other, so my parents suspect nothing. After a few weeks of coming by my family accepts his presence and engage him in conversation about church happenings and life in general. Both parents are out of the house one Sunday afternoon when he pays a visit. We talked, laughed and felt very comfortable with each other. After a while the others drifted away leaving us alone. The conversation becomes intimate and upon his suggestion we climb the stairs leading to the bedrooms. I sense danger, but allow myself to be reassured that it was okay to be alone in my parents' bedroom with him. Sitting on the bed, he begins caressing and kissing me, telling me how beautiful I am. As the caresses become more intense, I become frightened of impending danger.

"We can't do this," I said, trying to dissuade him. Being ten years my senior, he convinces me that it will be all right. I get caught up in the fervor of his passion, and before long we are having sex, on my parents' bed. This is the first, and only, sexual encounter between us.

"We are assured and know that all things work together and are for good and for those who love God and are called according to his design and purpose.

For those whom he foreknew, He also destined from the beginning to be molded into the image of His son that he might become the firstborn among many brethren."
Romans 8: 28-29 (AKJV)

# The Odyssey of Survival

***Life question:*** *Do we really know who we are? Is there a way for us to be sure we are who we are told we are? But who are we – is it our given names that identify us, that make us belong? And belong to whom? Our parents brought us into the world, but are we dependent upon them for our identity? Or do we belong to our creator? And if we do shouldn't we be called by his name? Most of us walk around seizing every opportunity to proudly rattle off the names of our parents and any connections we might have with any semblance of success. We 'name drop' to give the impression of belonging or at least know important people. But the question remains. Who are we, to whom do we belong? Do you know who you are?*

**Answer:**

## Chapter Nine

## SEVENTEEN AND PREGNANT

Twenty short minutes after he leaves the home, my parents return. I beg God to conceal from them what had so recently taken place on their bed. I am scared to look them in the face, believing that for sure my sin is planted on my forehead for them to see. God answers my prayers, because they remain ignorant of my actions. But that answered prayer is short lived. The second worst thing that could ever happen in my life becomes fact. My gut wrenching agonized cries to God, begging him not to allow it to be so, goes unanswered. My suspicion becomes real; in two months I realize I am pregnant. Nothing that has happened in my life up to this point, not the betrayal of my mother, the rapes, or the beatings, nothing prepared me for the shocking reality of my pregnancy. Never before had I prayed so hard for something not to be, but to my agonizing fate, it is so, and no amount of praying, wishing, and crying or anything else can save me from certain death. I am seventeen and pregnant. For weeks I hide my morning sickness from the entire household, pretending to gag on something when nausea rises in my throat in the mornings. I wish for death every moment of every day. I tell Henry of my predicament, and he promises to support me in every way. I do not want his support; I want to die. To my horror my flat teenage stomach begins to grow. Now I'm really in trouble. How much longer will I be able to conceal this from my parents? I have no confidence even in my father's love. I'm totally alone in this. If a person could cry to death, I would have succumbed to its icy fingers. To make matters worse Henry decides to tell my parents about the situation. Even after much begging and pleading for him not to carry out his plans, he remains adamant to do the right thing. One evening he shows up at our house. I run upstairs and lock myself in a bedroom fervently begging God to take my life then and there. He doesn't answer my prayer.

## The Odyssey of Survival

With ears glued to the keyhole I listen as my parents are told that I was pregnant. The house is suddenly as still as the forbearing calm before the storm. My heart leaps into my throat; pounding so hard I hear it in my ears. Trembling in fright, shaking like a leaf, I cried out to God.

"God what is going to become of me?"

Expecting to hear my mother shout my name, I listen, dreading the sound of her voice. Instead, an equally frightened sister knocks on the door, telling me mother had called me. She takes one look at me and starts crying. She knows what I already knew. I was dead. On wobbly legs and with downcast eyes I enter the room. If looks could kill I would have died on the spot from the venom which spouted from my mother's eyes. I don't know what to do. Should I sit? Stand? Next to whom? Even Daddy has turned against me; looking at him the disappointment in his eyes has dimmed the familiar sparkle. I lurk in the back of the room, as far away from everyone as possible.

"Is what I just heard true?" my mother barks at me.

Unable to speak and with eyes fixed on the floor. I nod. A litany of abuse spews from her mouth. She calls me every name in a truck driver's vocabulary book. I sink lower and lower into the ground. If only some higher being could have mercy on me causing the ground to open up and swallow me, but that didn't happen either. I have survived a great deal in my seventeen years, but not this time. There is no way out of this dilemma. When Henry gets up to leave, I beg him with my eyes, not to leave. At least while he is here I'm safe from the kicks and punches which I'm sure will come raining down upon my head. Without speaking directly to me, he walks out the door. His eyes speak volumes, but he knows better than to address me. My sisters, feeling my pain and shame share my discomfort as we watch his retreat. We fear for what will follow. What is she going to do to me? I have brought the ultimate disgrace upon the family.

# The Odyssey of Survival

To everyone's surprise she doesn't touch me, but I wish she would. People say, sticks and stones can break my bones, but words can never hurt me. But her words and actions towards me have broken more than my bones. My spirit, the zeal for life, my ambitions and dreams, everything has been taken away from me, and now I have committed the ultimate unforgivable sin, a sin that in a short time will no longer be a secret. People will begin talking about the family, and worst of all the church will become involved. What eludes me is that, after all the years of being raped by my godfather, pregnancy had not occurred. Now after just one encounter with someone else, here I am with a child growing deep in my womb. Mother refuses to speak directly to me, except to curse me every moment that I am in her presence. If we meet in the hallway, she shuffles back, holding her dress away from me in an effort to avoid contracting my leprosy. I am forbidden to have meals at the table with the family, and become an outcast in the household. Nothing, which has happened to me before, was as painful as this experience. I know I have done wrong, but does she have to treat me with such scorn and disdain? Daddy, after his initial shock and disappointment, tries to make me feel comfortable. They fight day and night over me, and I cry constantly. As my stomach grows; so does mother's hatred of me. My sisters suffer right along with me and they bear the brunt of her anger. I am hopeless and helpless and can take no more. To make the entire situation worse there is one huge disgraceful, insurmountable problem. Henry is married. The ultimate disgrace takes place two weeks later. Our parents are not home. Startled by a loud bang and raised voices we rush to the front door. Peering out the window we see to our horror Mavis, Henry's wife, accompanied by her mother, sister and brother. Metals meet as they banged on the gate with an iron pipe, yelling my name, daring me to come out so she could rip her husband's child out of me after killing me.

"Come out here Marcia Macaroon, you little whore! Come out so I can kick your ass. I want a piece of you. If you think you are a woman come out that door."

## The Odyssey of Survival

Oh God, no. Not this, anything but this. He had promised not to tell her about the pregnancy. Has he broken his promise the same way he promised that I would be safe?

"Little bitch you and that pickney will never be safe. I promise to kill both of you. Wherever you go for the rest of your life you had better look over your shoulders, because if its one day before I die, I will kill you."

"God why can't you just kill me now? This cannot be happening. I'll never be able to live this down. Please, I am guilty as charged. Please execute judgment against me and kill me now."

Her mother, sister and brother add their threats to hers. Bang, bang on the gate with a length of iron. The cussing, name-calling and threats continue for about an hour. I'm mortified; killed by shame. We're prisoners, fortressing ourselves behind the iron bars of the grilled gate and locked door. With every clang on the gate my distress grows. The barking dogs in the yard and jeers of the neighbors who gather to enjoy the free show kill everything in me. Again I beg God to rescue me by taking my life. How can I walk the streets again?

After satisfying them by calling me every conceivable name, bringing the neighborhood to the gate to glare, and sneer and laugh at us, they walk away, leaving me shaken, intimidated, and scared for my life. I'm too ashamed to ever walk out the door again.

"What happened to the gate, why is it all bent and twisted? Mother asks as she tries to open it to come into the yard. It takes the strength of four to release the lock.

"What happened here?" she asks again. None of us want to be the bearer of bad news, no one speaks.

"Marcia, what happened to the gate? I want an answer *now*."

# The Odyssey of Survival

With head hung low I explain that Mavis had come to the house cursing and hitting the gate with a piece of iron.

"See what you have brought upon the family? Look at the disgrace you have caused having a woman come to my gate to cuss you because you are carrying her husband's child. If I was here I would have opened the door and push you outside so she could beat you to death. Right now death is the best thing that could happen to you. How am I supposed to hold my head up in the neighborhood after this? Get out of my sight you disgusting thing. You make me sick."

Not as sick as I am. When will this come to an end? Finding the darkest corner in the house, I huddle there stroking my bulging stomach. My baby seems to sense the turmoil swirling around me. I whisper to her.

"I don't know what's going to happen to us sweetheart now I am scared to walk the streets because Mavis threatens to be behind every corner waiting for an opportunity to kill us. I don't know what to do. But I will give my life to protect you."

After a particularly hard night of listening to mother's hate and disgust at the sight of me, I tearfully informed my godfather of the situation at home. I'm desperate, and cannot continue living like this. I ask for his permission to remain at his home for a while. He says yes, at least until the tension at home calms down. I know that this was not going to be a good situation; but my decision is made based on the lesser of the two evils. I have endured enough from mother. Living conditions have become unbearable, my emotions are raw, and conflict is high. My mother hates the sight of me, the household is suffering because of me; my condition is a disgraceful evidence of my sin, in full view of all to see. They are all ashamed of me. I have to go. Returning home from work that evening I tell the chauffeur to wait for me, as I will be returning to the home with him. I tell Mother of my decision to leave the home, to which she promptly replied.

# The Odyssey of Survival

"Good riddance, don't bother coming back with your bastard pickney and I hope Newell kick you out too because you'll be a disgrace and embarrassment to him."

Daddy is not home, but he will be told when he comes home. My sisters cry at my departure, and my heart breaks with distress, but this has to be done. I can no longer live under the same roof with my mother in my present state. Taking up residence at my godfather's, is similar to making my bed in hell. On the first night of my arrival, the sexual abuse, which had abated, begins again. My pregnancy means nothing to him, and now that I'm completely at his mercy, totally dependent upon him for a salary, shelter and for food is almost worse than living at home. But the die has been cast; my decision has been made; now I had to deal with it. With gritted teeth and tears rolling down my cheeks, I endure him having his way with me nightly. I tell Henry where I am and he comes to visit. I'm careful not to mention the nightly assaults and convinced him that I'm safe. He calls frequently and assists with preparations for our baby's arrival.

Church has heard about my pregnancy, and instead of doing what I mistakenly think is the right thing, to help a sinner, who falls from grace find her way back, a church board meeting is called, and the decision is made that Henry and I will be disfellowshipped from the church membership; we will no longer be members of the denomination. This decision hurt almost as much as my mother's words. I cry my heart out. The place and people who the Lord had admonished to "Feed my sheep." Has just abandoned two sheep from the fold because they have fallen. I feel as if the last straw to which I am clinging to for dear life, the last place where I think God can be found has been taken away from me. I did not expect them to welcome me with open arms, but at least a visit from the pastor to talk about the situation may have helped my feeling of desolation. I have not only been severed from my parents and family, but also from church and from God. If this is the way church members are treated when they need the support of this extended family, then I want nothing more to do neither with them, nor, for that matter with their God. My mother has already tarnished any concept I may have had about a good God

# The Odyssey of Survival

who cares for his children, and now the church has administered the final blow. I have become an outcast. My life continues to be a living nightmare from which I cannot awaken. A trial had taken place, the jury has come in, and I have been sentenced to life in hell. There is little contact with my sisters, there are no friends to talk with, and none of my parents bother visiting me. My days are spent working, and nights are spent being raped. Crying because of pain doesn't matter, crying in despair doesn't help, begging God to rescue me by way of death isn't working, no one responds to my pleas. I'm helpless and no one cares enough about me to help or protect my baby or me.

One night I'm exceptionally tired of the unwanted sexual advances. I lock myself in the bedroom, hoping to keep him away. Lying there in fear, I don't know how he's going to react, but hope the locked door will dissuade his advances. When he tries the door finding it locked, he knocks. He calls my name, but I don't respond. He knocks again calling me again. I continue to feign sleep. I'm determined not to let him in. To my horror he delivers a few kicks to the door, kicking it right off the hinges. In fury he enters the room, wearing nothing but his underpants. Nervously I sit up in bed pulling the covers up to my chin.

"This is my house, and everything and everyone in it belongs to me to be used by me whenever I please. If you do not want to follow my rules then pack your bags and get out. But as long as you live here you will be available to me whenever I choose to have you. Do you understand that?"

Not waiting for an answer he roughly pushes me down on the bed, satisfies himself; while I bawl. I am delirious with distress and agonize daily about my situation. Where am I going to put my baby when she is born? The due date is fast approaching. It's to the point where my days are barely tolerable. I place one foot in front of the other; perform my duties, smiling accordingly. My heart has been torn to shreds and I'm miserable beyond words. At night, after he's finished with me, I hug my growing belly and apologize to my unborn child.

# The Odyssey of Survival

My only friend and companion was this little life growing inside of me. I hope it's a girl. I call her my little baby girl.

"It's just you and me against the world my precious little baby girl, just you and me against the world."

Nightly I repeat this phrase to her, growing strength from the fact that I have to protect her against the world. As she moves within me, my heart comes back to life. I fall in love. I love her unconditionally. I apologize to my baby for putting both of us at the mercy of the two people who have hurt me most in my life, but promise that somehow we will manage to rise above my present situation. One day I will be able to provide for my baby independently of them. I promise myself that if anyone ever tries to hurt or harm my baby I will go to prison for murder. The months pass and my delivery date is dangerously close. Passing each other on the steps one afternoon, my godfather, just as coldly as he had raped me tells me that I can no longer remain at his home because I have become a source of embarrassment to him. My steps falter, I hold onto the wall for support as my head swims from his words.

"Where am I supposed to go?" I ask him.

"I'm going to call your parents and tell them to come and take you home." He replied. "It's no longer appropriate for you to remain here."

I'm seven and one half months pregnant. I lock myself in the room and cry and cry and cry. Why couldn't God have mercy on me and deliver me from this for good? What am I going to do now; there is no way I'm returning home to the scorn and verbal abuse of my mother. I would rather die first. But death did not visit me that night. Two evenings later my parents arrive. I'm shocked to see them, as no one had bothered to tell me that they were coming. I promptly hide myself in my room. They have not seen me in months and I cannot face them. They talk for a while, and suddenly there's a knock on the door that startles me. Before I can answer, it opens and my angry mother enters the room.

# The Odyssey of Survival

"Look at you," she spits in contempt. "A total disgrace and a big failure. Everybody had such high hopes for you, and look at you, breeding for a married man at seventeen. You are a disgrace to the family and to your godfather. I don't want you back in my house and your godfather doesn't want you here any longer, so what are you going to do now?"

With my face turned to the wall and eyes swollen almost closed from crying, I frantically try to figure out what to do. I give serious thought to getting one of his guns (he keeps two in his room) and shoot myself. But what if I succeed in killing myself but my baby survives? What will become of her? No, regardless of what happens to me, I have to remain alive for her sake, to protect her from the world. I will survive this at any cost. After telling me how much she despises me she leaves the room, and I cry some more. My father who I thought loves me so much does not bother looking in or speaking to me. I guess he is too ashamed of me to look at my face. A household help comes to tell me to pack my belongings and go home with my parents. In astonishment, I look at her.

'I'm not going." I said.

"Miss Marcia they told me to tell you to get ready."

"I don't care what they say. I am not going"

She leaves the room shaking her head. I lock it and bawl loudly not caring who hears me. No, no, no, I was not returning home with them, I would rather become homeless. They hear the disturbance and my mother returns to the door.

"Open the door." she orders.

"No" I continue screaming. No amount of talking can get me to move, he will have to kick the door in again. They try talking to me from the other side of the door and I stubbornly refuse to budge. Finally they leave me alone returning home. He leaves me alone that night too. But my reprieve is short lived. The following day, while I work in the office, unknown to me, he orders the help to pack my belongings and have the chauffeur place them in the car trunk. At the end of the work day when I returned to my room, it's empty of my things.

"What happened to my stuff?"

I ask the help who's walking with me along the hallway.

"I'm sorry Miss Marcia, but Mr. Newell told me to pack them up and put them in the car so the chauffeur can take you home."

I'm dumbfounded. How can he do this to me?

I lock myself in the bathroom crying. Minutes later when I come out he is calmly leaning against the wall with arms folded across his chest waiting for me.

"You have to go home," he tells me. "The car is waiting for you and the chauffeur has to go home, so hurry up. It's close to your due date and I can't keep you here any longer. Don't worry about work. We'll manage without you until after the baby is born. I'll send you your salary as usual. Your job will be here when you are ready to come back. Now go and take care of yourself. Good-bye".

With those words I'm escorted out the door and into the waiting car.

"Have you not known? Have you not heard? The everlasting God, the Lord, the Creator of the ends of the earth, does not faint or grow weary; there is no searching of His understanding.
He gives power to the faint and weary, and to him who has no might. He increases strength.
Even youths shall faint and be weary.
But those who wait for the Lord shall change and renew their strength and power, they shall lift their wings and mount up as eagles, they shall run and not be weary, they shall walk and not faint or become tired.
Isaiah 40: 28-31 (AKJV)

***Life question:*** *The most beautiful Lilies can be found in the murkiest water. Beauty comes out of ashes, the oil of joy from mourning, and a garment of praise for the spirit of heaviness. Out of all this came the most beautiful, loving, caring child a mother could have ever wished for. She has absolutely nothing to do with the hardships I endured. Since giving birth to my first child, it has not ceased to amaze me how any mother could treat their children the way we were treated. If I had the opportunity to relive my life and had the option of choosing to go through exactly what I had gone through to have my daughter, or to have the life we craved, without my child. With no hesitation I would have chosen my child. Would you?*

**Answer:**

## *Chapter Ten*

## SURVIVAL

Up to this point in my life, I thought I had lived through hell, but the reality is that what has happened before was only a foretaste of how cruel my mother can be. Compared to the treatment meted out to me upon my return home, I had been a cherished child before. Of course I did not expect to be greeted with open arms and a welcome home banner strung across the front porch, after all I had done wrong and had broken all the rules, bringing unwanted scrutiny and shame on the family. I'm a disappointment and an embarrassment to my parents and to my siblings, they have to answer questions about my condition, and church members treat them almost as badly as they treated me, almost to the point of holding them responsible for my actions. The neighborhood looks on with curiosity, waiting to see what will happen to the pregnant teenage daughter of this home, where the children had not been allowed to mingle with their children, because our mother behaved as if we are better than them. Little do they know we are the most ill treated and abused in the entire neighborhood. The drive home seems too short. I do not have enough time to sort out my thoughts, to devise a plan of action, to think about the sudden change of circumstances. This could not be happening, the night before I was unable to face them. How am I going to live with them? My stomach is huge, so there is no disguising the problem. My baby moves within me, and tears instantly spring to my eyes. It's as if she senses the tension and uncertainty and is trying to reach out and reassure me that it was going to be okay. But was it really going to be okay? Would we survive my mother?

How am I going to protect my baby?

With butterflies in my stomach, trembling hands and tears in my eyes, I sit silently in the car willing the chauffeur to continue driving. But he stops the car, looks back at me and announced that we are here. He walks to my side and opens the door for me to leave the safety of the car. Slowly, I shuffle my body to the door trying to prolong the inevitable for a few more seconds. One of my sisters notices the car at the gate with me sitting in it. Excitedly she cries my name running to greet me. She takes a long look at my swollen stomach and hugs me telling me how much she has missed me. Mother, hearing the voices, comes to see what's going on. Her eyes narrow into slits and her hands go akimbo. I'm scared to venture into the gate, but my suitcases have been removed from the car trunk and the chauffer is carrying them through the gate. My sister softly encourages me to come on. She senses the fear in my hesitation as my steps falter and my head goes down.

"She can't do anything to you."

My sister whispers in my ears, but in my heart I know better. Mother can do a lot to me and to my unborn baby. At this moment I'm more scared of her than I have ever been in my life. Timidly I walk toward the door. She watches me without saying a word. I approach the steps. She flings her arms down in exasperation, spit in the grass, and whirl around huffing away. I'm crushed; nothing has changed in the five months I have been away. My father and other siblings are happy to have me back. To make my life a little easier, daddy says that I can have a newly added room to the house as my room, so my baby's crying will not disturb the family at nights. I like this arrangement, and am thankful for small mercies. Henry bought a crib and other items, which are already in the room. Is it possible for a seven and one half months pregnant teenager to remain invisible? I have to find a way to do just that. I learn to stay out of my mother's way. I observe her movements and move around only when she is out of the house or in another part of it. Her scorn of me is so great that if our paths cross at the same point she reverses her steps hastily walking in another direction. When she has no choice but to speak to me, she does so in the harshest tone possible. Constantly I am reminded of how awful I look, the failure and disappointment I am, and the disgrace I have brought on the household. She hates the sight of me and I try blending into the furniture to avoid her scrutiny. This is impossible.

# The Odyssey of Survival

One day she hears me telling one of my sisters to put her hand on my stomach to feel the baby's movements. She quickly puts a stop to that, accusing me of encouraging my sisters to follow me in my lewd and disgraceful behavior. She takes no part in the preparation for the baby, but we are able to acquire all the necessary items. In her absence we lovingly wash, fold and pack away the tiny garments, daydreaming about the baby.

Amelia and Victoria hear about the situation and visit us from Canada. We are delighted to see them. They encourage me and talk to mother about her treatment of me. This only makes the situation worse. They tell me I'm the first child to become pregnant while living in the home and give me credit for surviving her venom. They spend a week giving us their contact information before leaving. My baby will soon be born. I have to stop worrying about my survival and focus on the life of my innocent child about to be born into this dysfunctional family. Regardless of the cost, this child will be protected and loved and cared for. She will be kept out of the clutches of the evil that have been a part of our lives. Daddy is silent during this entire episode. He disapproves of my behavior, is disappointed about what has happened, but he is never cruel to me. He speaks to me in normal tones and tries to help me bear the wrath of mother. Secretly he slips me money to help prepare for the baby and even asks how I feel. He has to be careful not to be caught showing any attention to me, or he will be accused of condoning my behavior. Nevertheless he endures hell from her, especially at nights when she thinks we're asleep.

"I was right." I overhear her say to Daddy one night. "All the money we wasted on her sending her to school could have been put to better use. See she end up as nothing just as I predicted."

"The child made a mistake. That does not mean she is worthless."

"She is worthless, no better than a dog. I hate the sight of her. I should have taken a coat hanger to her, ripping the bastard pickney out of her so I wouldn't have to look at her now."

# The Odyssey of Survival

"You are crazy. She is not the first person to get pregnant. Give her a chance I'm sure she'll make something out of her life later. Don't be so hard on her. All I ever see her do is cry. She is sorry for what happened."

"Take up for her all you want. If you were a better father this would not have happened. You always defend them so they think they can do whatever they want and get away with it. Well not this time; as soon as she pushes out that baby she had better find somewhere else to live. I'm not having them live in here with me."

Where do you expect her to go?"

"I don't give a damn, just as long as she is out of my sight."

Daddy defends me. But his defense is useless. I cover my mouth with my hands in an attempt to stifle the agonizing cries, which rise in my throat. Those words burn a hole as deep as the Grand Canyon in my soul. I purpose in my heart, silently promising Daddy and myself. "Don't worry Daddy, I promise that if it's one-day before death's icy fingers claim me from this world, I will become somebody. Her prediction has to be proven wrong. If it takes my entire life I will show her that I am worth something. Thank you for trying to take up for me."

I'm almost ready to give birth and am very uncomfortable. On my last doctor's visit, Henry met me at the doctor's office (he had been forbidden to visit the home). He promises to visit me in the hospital; willing to disregard my mother's orders to stay away from me. He wants to see his child. I do not know what to expect in the delivery room and am scared, but I'm ready to deliver my baby. Maybe if my mother is not constantly reminded of what I had done each time she lays eyes on me my life may be a little easier. But then again, whoever said life is easy?

Sunday morning, September 15$^{th}$, the pains in my stomach wake me. After I sit up in bed for a few minutes, they subside. I try

## The Odyssey of Survival

returning to sleep and almost succeed when another sharp pain have me hugging my stomach, swaying back and forth, moaning. I don't know what to do, and I'm certainly not going to wake my mother. I try to make myself comfortable, nodding off when I can, rolling around groaning softly when the pain returns. At daybreak I take a shower returning to my bed as I wait for the household to awaken for the day. By this time I realize that I'm in labor, with contractions about fifteen minutes apart.

    One of my sisters is the first to come downstairs and enter my room to check on me. I tell her what has been happening and she gets my parents. A barrage of questions: how long have you been in pain? Why didn't you wake us? How bad is it? While the questions are coming, a contraction comes right along and everyone springs into action. We must get to the hospital. My sisters want to accompany us to the hospital but they are told no; they have to go to school. I'm helped into clothing, my packed bag retrieved and a taxi is called. In silence I sit next to my father as we drive to the hospital. When the contractions come, I silently squeeze his hand, gritting my teeth, biting my lips to keep from screaming. I have resolved one thing in my heart. If it kills me, I am not going to cry in my mother's presence. I do not care how terrible the pain is, she is not going to hear me cry to give her the satisfaction of telling me that I should have thought of this before doing what I had done. I'm not going to cry. Not only do I want to cry, I want to scream, to throw my head back, and allow the pain which swells up in my body, exploding somewhere in my inner parts, to be expelled through my throat. I want to throw my legs apart and beg somebody, anybody to please rid my body of this child, which was causing such unbelievable red-hot searing pain to rip through my body. I want somebody to hold me and tell me it's going to be over soon. Somebody to tell me they love me, encourage me to hang in there just a little longer. But there is no one. Not a sound is uttered, except for a moan as I allow my head to roll back swallowing what rises up in me. No sir, I'm not going to cry in her presence. Not even if it kills me. The taxi driver senses that he has to hurry. He careens through the morning traffic, hitting every pothole on the street of Kingston. Every hole brings a fresh wave of pain, but with some unseen help I stick to my resolve. We arrive at the hospital and I'm assisted out of the car into a wheelchair. My parents follow the nurse as she wheels me in to be registered. The pre-delivery preparation is completed. I'm in agony with contractions five minutes apart.

      In a few minutes they have me admitted and in a bed in the delivery room. At last I can succumb to the pain, which seem to have no end. A nurse comes in to check my vital signs, and as if on cue, my water breaks. I'm embarrassed, but she quickly puts me at ease. She gets help changing the bed linens, making me as comfortable as possible. My baby is about to be born. The pain is agonizing. Our future is uncertain, but I'm not going to worry about it now. I give myself over to what is happening, allowing this experience to take place. When this is over will we be all right? What is going to become of us? I have no idea.

"And do not be afraid of those who kill the body but cannot kill the soul, but rather be afraid of Him who can destroy both body and soul in hell.
Are not two little sparrows sold for a penny? And yet not one of them falls to the ground without your Father's consent and notice.
But even the very hairs of your head are all numbered.
Fear not, then, you are of more value than many sparrows."
Matthew 10: 28-32 (AKJV)

# The Odyssey of Survival

***Life question:*** *There are no easy answers to my life. Living in my mother's home means more than living through a situation. It means surviving her. Will my baby survive her wrath and hatred? Will I be able to protect her from the blows and verbal abuse we have endured our entire lives? What type of person would she grow up to be, beginning her life in this awful household? Will God continue forsaking us, or will he decide to have mercy on the innocent child by providing a way for me to get us out of this mess? How am I going to protect my daughter from my godfather?*

***Answer:***

## Chapter Eleven

## MY FIRST BORN

Monday, September 16th, 1975 seems to have no end. The day is spent in agony, first in the taxi, then thrashing around in a hospital bed with no comforting voice of love next to me. There is no one there offering a hand for me to squeeze, no one to wipe the sweat of labor from my forehead, assuring me it would be over soon. Alone, I cry, trying to find the strength to hang in there to give birth to my baby. I have no idea of the whereabouts of my parents and don't even care; I only know that I'm alone and in unbearable pain. As the day wears on I receive medication that helps me to relax and even lull me into a restless sleep, which last for a few minutes. The nurses and doctor keep a constant watch on me, commenting that I'm young and small and the first baby's birth of teenage mothers usually take longer. I find no comfort in those words; I only want to get it over and done with. But I'm powerless to speed up the process.

Exactly one month and fifteen days earlier I turned eighteen, and should have been in college somewhere, or in an office working at making a living and planning how to get out of my mother's house. Instead of planning a party to celebrate the beginning of adulthood, I'm in a hospital room waiting to give birth to a baby. This is not what I wanted, this is not what I planned or hoped for during my teenage years, but it happened, and regardless of who says or does what, this baby is going to be very special to me. She (I'm hoping for a girl) is going to receive so much love from me that she will not miss the love of a father or of anyone else that chooses not to love her. I will love her enough for the entire world. The pains become unbearable with only a couple minutes apart. The medical team gets active monitoring my progress. I'm transferred from one bed to another, crying out in the pain of being moved. Almost immediately my body feels as if it's

## The Odyssey of Survival

being ripped into a million pieces. The nurses get me ready in the birthing position telling me not to push until they tell me to. (I still wonder how they expect a woman in the throes of labor not to push). I try to follow the instructions, but my body wants to do otherwise. My young body begs for release as I scream with every push. As the life inside fights desperately to be released from the confines of her embryo sac, then the umbilical cord is cut, allowing her to breath on her own for the first time. The doctor and nurses try coaching me along. They announce she is coming, "her head is crowned." they said. I had no idea what that meant. The pressure to push is so great that I'm unable to control the urge; with every ounce of strength left in me I give a huge push, experiencing instant relief, as they joyfully announce.

"It's a girl!"

Instantly I forget about the last eighteen hours of agony. My little baby girl has been born. As they clean her up I try to get a glimpse of my daughter but they still have work for me to do. I have to wait a few more minutes to see her. As soon as they are finished with the details they put me in an upward position, and gently put my baby in my arms. It's the happiest day of my life. While cradling my baby and looking into her beautiful face, a fresh wave of tears wash over me. This time they are tears of joy. Checking to see if she has ten fingers and ten toes, I hold her close to me kissing her. A love I did not know existed, flows through me. My heart races with love for her from every fiber of my being. Only death can separate us. I love her enough to fight the world for her, and if necessary give my life for her. I love her with an everlasting love, a love that knows no end. In those first moments of meeting my daughter for the first time, I know that there is nothing I will not do for her. I can't get enough of her. Quietly she sleeps in my arms. The nurse comes in to take her to the nursery.

"No." I protested. "Please let me keep her with me."

"You have to get your rest." She tells me.

"You just did a great deal of work and need to recover, don't worry we'll bring her back later, now get some rest."

I relinquish her, following the retreating nurse with my eyes through the door. Not realizing how exhausted I am, I stretch out on the bed falling asleep.

I awake to the sound of voices, a porter tells me that he's moving me to another room, and that it was visiting time. A few minutes later my baby is brought to me. I'm told to put her to my breast for her to begin getting used to sucking. She latches on to my breast and I get the biggest thrill out of the experience. My own little baby has arrived and is now totally dependent upon me for sustenance. Will I be able to provide for her? What an angel she is, absolutely beautiful, perfect in every way. Her skin is of the finest velvet, her face as smooth and beautiful as the rising sun. Her big black eyes are like the morning stars shining in all their glory. Her cheeks have been kissed by God himself and she glows from the encounter. She smells like the aroma from the most expensive perfume house in France. All seven and a half pounds and twenty-one inches make her, without a doubt, the most beautiful baby to ever have been born into this world. I love her.

Visiting hours begin and in come my parents. For the first time in my life I do not care what my mother thinks or says. Nothing she says today is going to have any effect on me. They ask how I am as they examine my baby. I wonder if my mother expects her to have two heads and one eye. Cautiously she pulls back the blanket peeking at her. I watch her face for a negative reaction, and I'm stunned into silence when she announces that she is a beautiful baby. Inwardly I smile. She is beautiful, but I know better than to agree with my mother. Moments later Henry arrives. He enters the room, looks around and heads directly for my bed. I want to proudly display our baby, but my mother is present, watching my every move, so I calmly hand his daughter to him.

# The Odyssey of Survival

He takes one look at her and the biggest smile I had ever seen covers his face,

"What a beautiful little girl." He kisses her, holding her close. He is proud of his daughter.

Our hospital stay lasts for two days. My parents do not return the second day but Henry does. Without their presence, he sits and we talk. I have never told him about the hardships I endured during the pregnancy, nor about any of the abuse by my mother and godfather. He asks if I had been okay, and I simply reply, "I'm fine." This is probably a mistake, maybe if I had told him about the situation at home he would provide a home for us, but I'm confused and ashamed of my life. I feel that telling him may drive him away, so I keep my mouth shut. I don't know what we're going home to. But whatever happens, somehow we will survive. On the third day of her birth we are discharged from the hospital. The hospital porter wheels us through the front door. There is no one waiting to take us home.

"Who is going to pick you up?" He asks.

"No one" I replied.

"Would you like me to get you a taxi?" He asked,
"Yes" I replied.

He hails a taxi; we're bundled into it and the journey of uncertainties begins. I arrive at my parent's home, but there is no one there. I neither have a key or money. What am I going to do? A neighbor looks out noticing my predicament. She offers to pay the taxi driver, invites me to wait on her porch for someone to come home. Gladly I accept the offer sitting down while the family looks at my baby, all exclaiming how beautiful she is. Shortly afterwards my mother arrives home. My suitcase is sitting inside the gate. She notices it. Knowing no one is home she looks around for me. She sees me sitting on the neighbor's porch.

# The Odyssey of Survival

I begin gathering my baby's blanket around her to go home. She is furious. I cross the street. She lashes out at me.

"What makes you so proud of your bastard Pinckney that as soon as you get home you have to go to people's house to show it off?"

"I'm not showing her off". I tried explaining." But there was no one home and I don't have a key so she offered me a seat on her porch until someone came home.

"You should just sit down on the steps over here. You have nothing to be proud of."

Blinking back tears, I suck in my hurt feelings; hug my baby a little tighter saying not one more word.

"Look at you." she continues, "A baby in your arms and no husband at your side. Your father and I have to take on this responsibility as if we don't have enough mouths to feed. Get inside; I hate the very sight of you."

Things are going to be tough, life is going to be difficult…but some way, somehow we will make it. What I have failed to understand is my mother's animosity and berating of me because I'm unmarried. I know Henry is married and I'm ashamed of that. For a long time she refers to my baby as a bastard. Has she forgotten that it was her doing that introduced my sisters and me to sex at the young age of twelve? Has she forgotten how she lied about Patricia's paternity? Has she forgotten that all five children born to her and Daddy had been conceived and born out of wedlock? Has she forgotten that she is no paragon of virtue?

Thankfully, the rest of the family arrives home soon. My sisters are ecstatic and welcome their niece into the family. From that day forward my baby, whom I named Jessica Anita, became the love of everyone's life. She is a sweetheart of a baby, crying only when her needs are to be met. In no time she is laughing and playing, winning

# The Odyssey of Survival

every heart in the household. Even mother falls in love with her. Her personality is infectious; she is a pure joy to behold. Her father visits often, delighting in her. As soon as she is old enough to sit up he puts her on his shoulders taking her for walks throughout the neighborhood. My Daddy loves her and gets immense pleasure from bouncing her on his knees. Life at home becomes a little easier. Mother and I clash often, now we disagree over the rearing of my child. I will be dammed if I'm going to allow her to have any significant input in Jessica's life. We live in her home but I'm determined to raise my child without her influence.

Jessica is six months old. Mother informs me that the church board has decided that Henry and I are eligible for rebaptism since there has been no evidence that we have continued having a relationship. The event will take place two weeks later. I have no interest in being rebaptized or resuming church attendance. I harbor no desire to become a new spectacle, or the new topic of gossip, but mother tells me that if I do not comply with the decision of the church I cannot continue living under her roof. Two weeks later I dutifully show up at church and we're both dipped into the pool. I guess by this action they have rewritten my name on the church roll, giving God permission to re-admit me into heaven. The truth is I hate the entire bunch of them. I hate my mother, I hate the church and I hate the church members.

Now that I have been cleansed of my sins, my baby can be "blessed" in the holy sanctuary. The date is set for next Sabbath. I refuse to attend the service. On Sabbath morning my parents take Jessica to church while I remain home, fuming about all the hypocrites who will be feigning happiness for us, making their snide remarks, admiring her only to have our names as the main course over Sabbath lunch. Breaking under pressure from mother to attend church, I go. The stares and whispers are so long, loud and scornful that after a few weeks I refuse to resume regular attendance. The atmosphere is just too uncomfortable. I don't care what my mother says; I'm not going back. Daddy tells her to leave me alone, but she tells him to stay out of it. At her insistence I accompany them one Sabbath morning.

# The Odyssey of Survival

Entering the property, I can't believe my eyes. My steps falter – coming to a halt. There, right smack in the front entrance, surrounded by a full entourage leading the family into battle was Mavis, her mother, sisters and brother at her side. How did they know that I would be here today? Fear grips my heart. I clutch Jessica to my chest, refusing to proceed further. She notices us. Mavis breaks away from her gang coming directly at me. She bellows obscenities, threatening to kill us on the spot. Daddy places his arms around me. Mother glares at me yelling.

"You are never going to stop being a disgrace to this family. Are you? Now I can't even go to church in peace. Why can't you just die? If she wants to beat you right here you deserve it. Get the hell away from me."

Daddy defends me. "To get to her you are going to have to go through me. Leave her alone. What is done is done. Stop harassing her. She made a mistake. As a matter of fact your husband is the adult in this mess. He is a married man who should have known better. Have you asked him what was he doing with my 17-year-old daughter?" You need to deal with him. She is trying to go on with her life. Leave my daughter alone."

Tears run down my face dropping onto my sleeping baby's blanket. With a few choice words Mavis turns on her heels returning to the churchyard fuming, and cursing, protesting my presence at the top of her voice. Slowly we bring up the rear as the deacons and members come out to see what the commotion is about. I just want to get away, but my mother forbids me to leave.

"You brought this upon yourself. Now deal with the consequences. For the rest of your life you'll have to hide from her so get used to it. I have to put up with these indignations and insults. Everyone is talking about me behind my back all because of you. Now go find a seat in church."

# The Odyssey of Survival

"That's why I didn't want to come. You make me. Why can't I go home?'

"Shut up and go inside. It's your fault and your disgrace, deal with it."

Finding a seat in the back, I perch on the edge of the bench. My eyes never stop scanning every direction. The enemy is on the same property. We are in danger. My fears are not unfounded. Shortly after I sit down, the pack comes charging around the corner in search of their prey. Hunching low, I ease myself, with my baby in my arms into the farthest corner. Their eyes scan the congregation for a glimpse of me. They are out for my blood. Like the children of Israel marching around the city of Jericho to topple it, so the clan storms around the building looking for me. The elders and deacons try their best to restore peace to the scared grounds, but it's useless. The pastor takes control of the situation herding them all into his office while I hide in the back. They charge out of his office yelling insults at the minister.

"I have every right to be here! She should not be allowed on the property. What type of church are you running harboring the likes of her? We are not leaving. Find her and make her leave. She is the slut."

Mavis has been trying to get her hands on me and now she has me in sight. She smells my blood in her nostrils and was not giving up. I'm scared to death. A deacon notices me and quietly ushers me into the office.

"Be quiet." He admonishes. "If she can't find you she'll eventually leave."

My life flashes before my eyes. I have no hope. How can I live like this? I'll never be safe again. Holding my baby tightly I beg God to strike us both dead, to release the innocent little angel I am holding from this mess.

"Lord I can't go on. I am scared, embarrassed and petrified. My family is suffering because of me. My mother hates me even more, if that's possible. Please have mercy on us and take our lives now, I'll never be able to live a normal life. My baby will grow up with this stigma on her. She doesn't deserve it. She has done nothing wrong. Help us Lord, help us out of this."

But He doesn't answer me. The service has been disrupted with everyone enjoying a free show. They snicker and laugh talking about me, taking sides with Mavis and her family. I am the enemy of the entire congregation, I brought sin and its repercussions in their midst. I am doomed. The din outside subsides. Slowly the door opens and the deacon enters. With a sympathetic look on his face, he says.

"It's safe now. They left."

"No. I am too ashamed. Everyone is talking about me I can't face them."

"Okay. Stay here until the service ends, I'll tell your family where you are."

"Thank you."

At the end of the worship service I leave the room on wobbly legs, with down cast eyes and tear streaked face. Baby in arms I walk away from the New Haven SDA church. I will never return. I purpose in my heart that if there is a God who loves and cares for me and my baby he will have to find a way to convince me to come back to him. He will have to give me a reason to go back to church. God himself will have to appear to me to make me want anything to do with the things pertaining to him. From this point on I begin living my life without giving any thought to God.

# The Odyssey of Survival

"I will confess and praise you for you are fearful and wonderful and for the awful wonder of my birth! Wonderful are your works, and that my inner self knows right well.

My frame was not hidden from you when I was being formed in secret, intricately and curiously wroth in the depths of the earth.

Your eyes saw my unformed substance, and in your book all the days (of my life) were written before ever they took shape, when as yet there was none of them.

How precious and weighty also are your thoughts to me, O God! How vast is the sum of them."

Psalm 139: 14-17

**Life question**: *Was my mother correct in treating me the way she did? Did I have anyone to blame for my actions but myself? Should the church have acted in a more understanding way or were they also right in the way they handled my sin? Is this the way God instructs the Righteous to deal with the unrighteous sinner. But which one of us, by virtue of himself, is righteous? Didn't God himself say none is righteous, no not one? Did He not say He came to call sinners to repentance? Or was my sin beyond forgiveness?*

**Answer:**

## Chapter Twelve

## RAPE AND UNCONSENTED ABORTION

This is not my first choice but, for a fee, she decides that no one can do a better job of caring for her grandchild than she can. Against my better judgment I agree to the plan, thinking that since Jessica is a toddler there is not much harm that can be inflicted upon her. Mother knows better than to physically abuse her. Daily when I get home from work I scrutinize Jessica's entire body looking for marks or bruises.

Jessica grows into a beautiful, intelligent little girl. At four months she begins teething. At seven months she takes her first step saying her first words at eleven months. She has truly become a blessing in the home. Even mother dotes on her. My life is now centered on her. Everything I do is done with her welfare in mind. I'm accused of spoiling her. I certainly spoil her, but so does everyone else. I want to leave my parents home and provide for both of us on my own, but I'm not making enough money to make us independent yet. So I continue living here, working for my godfather and saving what I can. I have had no relationship of any type with a man, so when Jessica turns one year old and I become pregnant again I know who has to be the father. After returning to work things are good for a while. He leaves me alone for a couple months. Its election time and we have to travel to the parish he represented in the Island. The trip requires us to spend five days out-of-town. As his personal assistant, I have to accompany the team on the trip. It's distressing leaving my baby but I trust my sisters to take care of her for me. The obligations of the job have to be met, for the first time in her life I have to leave my baby for five days.

# The Odyssey of Survival

At the end of the first day in St. Thomas we all retire to bed. Thinking I'm safe in my room I neglect to lock the door and am awakened to the presence of someone getting into bed with me. I try jumping off the bed, but he is poised above me, pinning me to the bed. I thrash around, kicking my legs, trying to escape his clutches. He holds me in a tight grip, refusing to release my arm. I beg him not to do what I know he intends to do. I begin crying, begging him to stop, but he simply ignores my pleas and like old times, he rapes me. I spend the rest of the night crying. I'm back at square one. For a while I had began to feel like a normal human being, but those feelings have been dashed. My godfather had only been waiting for the right opportunity to assault me again. I'm a little older now, have given birth to a baby, and although I am still vulnerable to him and am still subjected to my mother's rules, I am stronger and will no longer silently succumb to them. The following night I try to lock the door and find that the lock didn't work. I suspect it have been tampered with making it impossible to keep him out. Of course he comes in raping me again. During the next day I secretly ask the maintenance man to take a look at the lock and fix the problem. He obliges. I still worry though because a little thing like a lock has failed to keep my godfather at bay before.

The third night I carefully lock the door. A little later I hear him trying to enter the room but finds the door locked. He curses under his breath and goes back to his room. I prop a chair under the doorknob trying to make sure I'm safe for the night. I drift off into restless sleep filled with nightmares. Work the next day is strained. I am red eyed from crying and try avoiding him except when it's necessary for work. Others join us the fourth day with a few of them deciding to spend the night there after working late into the night. When the meeting finally breaks up and we separate to retire for the night, I discover that a new arrival has been given my room. I ask the help why and where I am supposed to sleep? She tells me that Mr. Newell told her to give my room to the guest. I therefore need to speak with him. He is still entertaining a few male guests so I sit down in a corner reading a book while I wait. He excuses himself from the group to visit the restroom and I confront him.

## The Odyssey of Survival

"Uncle Duke, Gina tells me that you told her to give my room to a guest. All the other rooms are full. Where am I supposed to sleep?"

With a sinister smile he replies. "You will be sleeping with me tonight so go get ready and wait for me in bed until I come in." I'm in shock. How low will he go?

This man is a leader in the community, who is a minister in the country's government, who everyone looks up to. People thinks he is a good man, helping them to get their lives together, providing jobs for the people, making laws which affect the lives of the entire nation. A person with enormous power, and great wealth, who can with the stroke of a pen or one telephone call, change lives for the better or worse. He is a tyrant, a rapist and a horrible individual who wields his power over everyone. He is used to getting whatever and whomever he wants. A person who is once again trying to convince the people to vote for him, to give him another five years at the helm of the country to work and provide stability for them. This same man had viciously raped me at the age of twelve and for several years after. He has raped the other girls in my family, have raped and have continuous sexual encounters with many other teenage girls who I have witnessed in his bed on many occasions. This man of power, who is my godfather, has devised a plan to make me available to him. Not risking the chance that I will lock the door against him again, he leaves me with no place to sleep except in his bed so he can have his way with me all night. Well he is not going to have his way tonight. I'm no longer going to silently lie down and allow him to violate me anymore. I'm going to fight for myself. If he fires me then, so be it. He has taken advantage of me for so long that it has become a way of life for him. I decide that if he forces himself upon me one more time I'm going to reveal his true nature to someone. I am going to tell the wife of one of our founding fathers of the political party which he represented. I am going to tell Lady Balata, wife of Armando Balata, who is a frequent visitor to his home. I am very tired of his advances and decide to throw caution to the wind. Damn the consequences.

## The Odyssey of Survival

    I walk away from him. I will spend the night on the couch. Patiently I wait until everyone leaves the home. Calmly I make myself comfortable on the living room couch. When he realizes that I was not in his bed he comes looking for me. Finding me on the couch he tries persuading me to come to bed. But I'm adamant. After much talking he comes to the realization that I'm not going to budge. My mind has been made up, if he gets physical with me, I will scream bringing the guests out of their rooms to find out what's going on. Sensing my determination not to cooperate, he tells me how disappointed he is in me, huffing off to his bed. I couldn't care less how disappointed he is in me. So was my mother and father and I didn't care. I have been abused enough and have to take a stand at some point in my life. I realize that if I continue allowing him to take advantage of me, this cycle will never end. I have survived him for years, have survived my mother for years, have survived a pregnancy, and now have a child to live for. The victim that I had become needed to stop being afraid of the consequences, and put up boundaries in her life. This is the first one to go up. I may have to pay dearly for it because I know how calculating and cruel he can be to those who dare to deny him what he wants. But I don't care, he can't kill me so let him do whatever he wishes. The business in St. Thomas is completed and we return to Kingston. I'm dropped off at my home, delighted to see my baby as she comes running, flying into my arms. The problems of the past five days melt away as I embraced her, never wanting to leave her again. It's the weekend so I'm able to spend two days doting on her. Work on Monday resumes as usual, with no discussions, but there have never been any discussion about the rapes. It amazes me that no one ever speaks about anything that happens in that house. It's almost as if a code of silence has been placed upon everyone who enters the halls.

    Two weeks later, I'm surprised that my monthly cycle fails to make an appearance. With fear in my heart I wait to see what will happen as the weeks progressed. Maybe I'm just late. Four weeks later I'm still late, and much to my chagrin, I wake up with morning sickness.
    "Oh God no, this can not be happening, I can not be pregnant, and for whom? I'm really going to die this time."

# The Odyssey of Survival

I am devastated. It has only been one year since the birth of my daughter. Her father and I have never been intimate with each other again. I'm not even friendly with another man, so there is no doubt to whom this baby belongs. Trouble has just taken up permanent residence at my door. When my third period is missed, I know without a doubt that the most dreaded thing has befallen me again. I have told no one about my situation. At the end of a workday I lag behind waiting for the other workers to leave. I tell my godfather about my condition. Feigning innocence he begin telling me that he hopes the young man will stand up to his responsibilities, taking better care of me this time. Looking him in the eye I tell him.

"There is no young man, the baby is yours."

He vehemently denies that such a thing could be possible. I remind him of his assault on me in St. Thomas and tell him that was when it happened.

"I have been with no one else. *You* are the one who forced yourself on me in St. Thomas."

He continues denying paternity, but I quickly put a stop to his statement.

"I have no doubt about whom the father is, because I have been with no one else. I have not had sex with anyone since before the birth of my baby, so I know for sure that it's yours."

This must frighten him; he cannot allow it to be disclosed. I leave for home fighting for calmness as my mind races around and around trying to figure how on earth this is going to play out. I can see my baby and myself on the streets, because I'm under no illusion that my mother will continue keeping me at home during another pregnancy, just one short year later. A couple weeks pass and on a few occasions he asks if I still felt the same way about him being the 'Father of the fetus', as he chose to refer to the pregnancy. I tell him. "Yes, and there is nothing to change."

# The Odyssey of Survival

I'm getting very worried. In another month it will become evident that I am pregnant and all hell will break loose again. I lose weight from worry and sleeplessness. At about midday on Friday of that week, he tells me that he has made an appointment for me, with his doctor, Dr. Gripe, who is one of his best friends and confidant. He tells me he wants a confirmation of the age of the fetus so he could determine if it really belongs to him.

"That's fine with me. I need to see a doctor anyway." The chauffeur is instructed to take me to Dr. Gripe. He gives me a sealed envelope addressed to the doctor. Knowing of their friendship I think nothing of the envelope. I tell the nurse who I am and that I need to see the doctor to personally deliver correspondence from the Hon. M. H. Newell, Minister of Government. Dr. Gripe soon appears to greet me and I deliver the envelope to him. A nurse tells me to wait; I will be the last patient. "That's okay." I say making myself comfortable. The chauffeur leaves me.

The other patients have been seen, I'm the only one left in the waiting room. The good doctor himself comes out to greet me again. We know each other, having met on several occasions at social gatherings. He has even visited the home a few times, but I have never been one of his patients. He invites me into his office asking about the 'Man on the hill', I assured him he is fine. He then asks what he could do for me. I tell him of my suspicions of pregnancy. He ushers me into an examination room, instructs me to get undressed, and get on the examination table, he will be right back. I have been through a prenatal exam before so I know what to expect. I get on the table and wait. When he returns I notice he is carrying unfamiliar equipments in a dish but ask no questions. He places them on a tray, but I had no reason to wonder what they are for. He asks the familiar questions to verify pregnancy. I answer honestly. After the examination he verifies that I am pregnant and he needs to do a blood test to determine the age and predict the due date. I know this to be true, so I nod in agreement. He leaves me with my legs in the stir-up telling me not to get dressed yet. He wants to do another exam. Uncomfortable as it is I remain in this embarrassing position.

# The Odyssey of Survival

With his back turned he prepares a needle for what I think is to draw some blood for the tests. Instead I have no time to object as he turns around, quickly inserting the needle into my hip giving me a shot.

"Why did you give me an injection?"

"To make you comfortable."

"Comfortable for what?" I ask.

He offers no answer. I fight to form the question in my mind again, but can't quite get it together. I'm drifting off into semi-consciousness, somewhere between sleep and being awake, in a type of twilight zone. I don't know for sure how long I remain in that state. I am vaguely aware of him working between my legs. I feel pressure but am unable to fathom what's happening. When I revert to consciousness I notice that I am alone in the room. My legs are out of the stir-ups and I'm lying flat on my back. I must have fallen asleep because I have absolutely no recollection of anything except the memory of him working between my legs. A few minutes pass while I'm quietly lying there trying to figure out why I'm asleep on a table in a doctor's examination room. Not long afterwards he enters the room, asking if I was in pain.

"No, why would I be in pain?"

"Because I performed an abortion on you."

"What." I exclaimed. "I did not ask you to perform an abortion."

"Those are my instructions."

"Whose instructions? I simply asked for an exam to verify my pregnancy."

# The Odyssey of Survival

"Miss Macaroon, I followed the instructions you gave to me yourself. Now if you feel okay please get dressed I need to go home."

With that he leaves the room. Pressing my hands to my stomach I try to feel the spot from which my child has been yanked out of me without my permission. Tears course down my face. This man had just killed my baby without even the decency of telling me what he was about to do. I have not been given the opportunity to make an important decision. Now everything has truly been taken away from me. The fact that the pregnancy would be the cause of great problems and distress did not give them the right to abort it without my knowledge or consent. I am shaking with fury. Slowly I get dressed, not sure how I should feel after what just happened. He leaves a sanitary pad on the bed telling me to use it, as there will be some bleeding. I take his advice. Dr. Gripe escorts me to the door telling me to take care, then retreats into his office leaving me to find my own way home. I board a bus and get myself home. As soon as I get home I begin experiencing sharp cramps in my stomach. I cannot care for Jessica and ask my sisters to look after her for me. "What's the matter?" They ask. "I have cramps." I replied getting into bed. It's impossible to rest with a one year old who has not seen her mother all day, so I play with her in bed for a while. Thankfully it's Friday and the family always retired to bed early on Friday nights after worship, as there is no television watching or homework or any work done after sunset. The house quiets down for the night, I ask my sisters to take Jessica upstairs with them because I really have bad cramps. They comply bringing her back to me after she falls asleep. I'm in great pain. I take four Tylenols but they have no effect on the pain. Sweat pours from my face as I hug my body far into the night. Pain rips through my body. Labor pains had not been this intense. I begin feeling as if I'm going to die. With the pain comes a perfusion of bleeding. Nothing could stem the flow. The sanitary pads filled up fast as I drag myself to and from the bathroom.

# The Odyssey of Survival

The pain is unbearable. I have to get help. I cannot die from bleeding in front of my baby who wakes up from my groaning. She calls. "Mummy" and I instantly know I have to get help from my parents upstairs or I'm going to bleed to death. I take Jessica out of bed, set her down on the floor and tell her to go upstairs and get Mama.

"Go get Mama" I tell her. "Tell mama that mummy wants her."

She walks off repeating her instructions, but she is only one year old, and is afraid of the dark. She goes to the stairs but returns to me in fear of climbing the dark stairs alone. I try sending her again but realize she is too young to carry out such a mission.

"Okay." I tell her. "Come with mummy, we have to go get mama."

Tagging along behind me, I drag myself up the stairs with my blood dripping down my legs. I crawl up the eighteen stairs to my parent's bedroom. As I crawl up I contemplate what to tell them. One part of me wants to confide in them but another part warns me that I will be blamed for what had happened, so I could not tell them the truth. By the time I get to the top of the stairs I'm in so much pain I don't care who knows what, I just need help. I open my parent's door calling out to them, awakening them. They see me prostrate on the floor with Jessica standing next to me. They spring off the bed asking, "What's the matter with you?" They notice my bleeding and my father exclaims, "Oh my God what happened to you?" I make no reply, just said I'm in pain. My father helps me to my feet, sitting me up on the foot of the bed. My mother gets towels and tried stemming the blood flow. I feel a contraction and to my embarrassment a huge placenta, falls right through the legs of my underwear plopping on the floor for everyone to see. They are shocked. I am ashamed, but right now all of that has to wait. I still need help. My sisters hear the commotion and come to ask what's happening. They are promptly sent back to bed and told to close the door. They obey taking Jessica with them. The pain subsides after the placenta is expelled but the bleeding continues. For the first time my mother comes to my aid showing concern for me. She cleans me up and keeps asking me what was wrong. By now I have decided not to confide in her. I know the information would only be used against me later. So I close my mouth feigning ignorance of what had caused this pain and severe bleeding,

"Is this the first time your period is coming back since you had Jessica?" mother inquires.

I quickly take hold of that explanation, telling her yes. She seems satisfied with that answer.

I want to confide in my Mother. I want to tell her what Uncle Duke had done to me. I want to tell her about my heartaches and my hurts, but I must keep my mouth shut. She has never been my confidant. How can I start confiding in her now? He has not only gotten away with numerous rapes, now he had ordered the murder of a child and will get away with it. Maybe this is a good time to go to the police. But who will believe me? Certainly Dr. Gripe will not testify against him, and which police officer will dare to read him his rights and arrest him? When I'm able to move, daddy helps me downstairs to the bathroom, then back into bed. He makes me comfortable telling me to call him if I need help during the night. The experience is horrifying. I spend the rest of the night in mental agony. Earlier that day I had been violated in the most dreadful way, was left to find my own way home, had not even been given one painkiller, but had been sent home to deal with what follows an abortion. I realize that my life means nothing to these people; I'm simply a pawn to be used, abused and thrown away when my usefulness is over. My godfather has no problem raping me but as soon as the consequences of his action was about to be made public; he wields his power. Hate and loathing for this man wells up in me. The idea that the doctor's orders had been delivered to him by my own hands in the sealed envelope sickens me, and to make matters worse I'm expected to return to work on Monday, expected to function as if nothing out of the ordinary has happened.

On Monday morning I refuse to go to work. The car comes to pick me up and I send back a message saying I'm sick. In fact I am very sick, my temperature has soared to 105 degrees, I'm

## The Odyssey of Survival

hemorrhaging and I'm weak and lethargic. For three days I remain in bed, drinking tears, hugging my baby for companionship. For two weeks I stay away from work. The thought of facing him is so unbearable that I decide to look for another job. I go for a few interviews but when the employers discover for whom I work and that I had to give notice to leave his employment, they offer excuses for not being able to hire me. They are afraid of the consequences when he finds out that they have hired away one of his employees. I had a child to provide for, so I swallow my loathing and return to work

    Not one word is spoken between us about what had transpired. He briefly inquires if I'm feeling better and I say yes. Work resumes as normal. But I do not return to normal. I feel a void deep within me that nothing can fill. I always cry easily, but this tendency is magnified. At the sight of a baby I get teary eyed, and any conversation pertaining to childbirth brings on a deep longing within me. As the months pass I find myself constantly keeping track of where my pregnancy would be now and at the end of nine months I descend into deep private mourning for the death of a child whose life had so brutally ended. I need healing. I need to talk to someone. I'm listening to the radio and hear the revelations of three women who have had abortions. I have buried the abortion deeply. I think I have it under control but now the emotions rise to the surface bringing a new wave of hysteria. I call the radio station. I talk with the host revealing to her what I have been so ashamed of. I bear my soul to her telling her about the abortion and how responsible I feel for the baby's death. I'm devastated. Tears are blinding me. Talking helps my aching soul, but healing does not come that day. If anything, it serves to intensify my sorrow. Wiping my tears, I tell myself, "Come on Marcia don't let them see you cry, you can do this girl, you have to, and you have Jessica to think about." My life is never the same again. Hours are spent each night crying. My dreams are tormented. I dream of trying to find my daughter, something deep within me tells me it was a girl. In my dream she cries for me. Always I recognized the cries as that of my child, coming from a distance. I'm running through open and closed doors, down long hallways, down the street, through buildings, always looking, calling out to her, telling her.

## The Odyssey of Survival

"I am coming sweetheart, hold on, I'm coming."

Always running, but never getting to her. Her cries ringing in my ears; my arms longing to hold her; to put her to my breast and provide food and comfort; longing to put her on my shoulders and rock her to sleep. I want to look into her eyes, touch her cheeks with my fingers, kiss her forehead and change her dirty diapers. But I never find her. At times she seems to be close, I can sense her presence I can almost reach out and touch her. If only I could find her. Where is she? Why can't I find her? Looking around one more bend; peering into the face of children; calling out to her.

"I am coming baby, you'll be alright; mommy is coming to get you."

I'm jolted out of restless sleep. With tears running down my face, I enfold myself in my arms and rock myself, finding comfort in my empty arms. I cry out to God for help.

"O God, help me. I am pathetic and in need of your forgiveness and love. One of the children you gave to me is dead. I did not personally kill her, but I feel responsible for her death. I know the little angel is in heaven with you, may you comfort her, because I can't. Please care for her, and Lord, please forgive me for the part I played in snuffing out her life before she had an opportunity to take her first breaths. I am nobody, just a pitiful girl born into the worst family imaginable. You have no reason to hear me, or even help me, but for my child's sake, please have mercy upon her soul."

Shortly after this, one of my older sisters, Lynnette, decides to migrate to Canada to join the others. About one month before her departure from the island she asks me if I would like to occupy her apartment and take care of her three children until she's able to file and take them to Canada. This is the best offer I have ever had. This will give me the opportunity to move out of my mother's house.

# The Odyssey of Survival

"Yes, I'll be happy to move into your apartment. When are you leaving?"

All the arrangements are made and she leaves for Canada. I move in with my daughter. Caring for the three children is a pleasure. They are good children and I love them. The eldest daughter Deirdre is more like a younger sister than a niece. Our mother tries talking Lynnette out of leaving the children in my care, telling her that I can hardly care for my own child and myself so they should be left in her care. But Lynnette refuses the offer. She knows how cruel our mother is.

For the first time I experience freedom. I'm free of my mother's control and I have my own place. We settle in nicely and my little household is happy. But happiness does not last long. In a couple weeks my mother decides that regardless of what Lynnette wants, the children should have been left in her care. She does not want the children in her care because she loves them; it all comes down to money. From past experiences she knows that as soon as Lynnette begins working money will be sent back to Jamaica to care for the children and the thought of her not receiving these funds are unbearable to her. She has to get these children in her home.

One fine evening we are all at home enjoying a quiet end to a busy day and like a bad penny, there comes Mother. She orders the children to pack their stuff and get themselves to her home. They refuse. I refuse to let them go, reminding her that if their mother wanted them to be with her she would have left them with her. Nothing we say fazes her. She actually produces a belt and begins beating the children into obedience. Short of physically fighting her there is little I can do. There ends taking care of my nieces and nephew. Lynnette is furious when I call and tell her what happened, but no amount of talking will make mother send them back. They now live with their grandmother, but at least I still have my freedom. Jessica and I are doing fine on our own. I continue working. I even continue leaving her in her grandmother's care during the days, but with delight I pick up my baby and retreat to my own apartment at the end of each day. I am happy. Finally my life seems as if I am getting a handle on it. Making my own decisions, paying my rent, doing our laundry it's a little piece of heaven on earth. My sisters visit often and they too enjoyed the freedom from Mother's constantly watchful eyes. The biggest trill of all is when there is a disagreement between her and daddy, and she leaves him no dinner, he no longer has to purchase something from the store. He simply comes to visit me and I gladly feed him. He comes by often to get a little peace. When she discovers his whereabouts she fumes. But we have learned to ignore her.

    Henry visits us regularly; he has gotten divorced and begins asking me to marry him. But I refuse the offer. Too many unpleasant things have occurred, too many hurts, too many broken promises. I have survived the pregnancy without him at my side and now feel that I want to find my own way without him. He is a link to the past and I want a fresh start. I prefer to meet someone new, someone who I will not associate with the pain of the last few years. Maybe then I can find healing and some peace. I'm also a little afraid of how the tongues of the church members would wag, and cannot see myself being happy among them. Maybe if I voice my concerns he will make the necessary changes to make me comfortable and happy. But I had been so scarred that I just want a new beginning with new people. The future of my child and myself depends upon me being able to establish some sort of stability to our lives. As long as I continue working for the enemy I will continue to be violated. But hope has returned, it burns deep within my heart. One day we will overcome.

"Rejoice in the Lord always, gladden yourselves in Him; again I say, Rejoice.
Let all men know and perceive and recognize your unselfishness. The Lord is near.
Do not fret or have any anxiety about anything, but in every circumstance and in everything, by prayer and petition, with thanksgiving, continue to make your wants known to God.
And God's peace, which transcends all understanding, shall garrison and mount guard over your hearts and minds in Christ Jesus."
Philippians 4: 4-7

**Life question**: *It is only by the Grace of God that I survived that abortion. I sought no medical help, simply took pain-killers, drank lots of liquids and rested. I don't know what the result would have been if I had confided in my mother. I wanted to tell her so badly, it ached, but she had never been my confidant, how could I start confiding in her now? Uncle Duke had not only gotten away with numerous rapes, now he had ordered the murder of a child, and had gotten away with it. For the remainder of my life this will haunt me. What should I have done? Maybe this was a good time to have gone to the police. But who would have believed me. Certainly Dr. Gripe would not testify against him. And which police officer would have dared to read him his rights and arrest him? What would you have done differently? How would you have handled the situation?*

**Answer:**

## *Chapter Thirteen*

## DEATH OF ANOTHER CHILD

A few months later I meet a handsome young man. We exchange telephone numbers and begin calling each other. He likes partying, and we become a couple. We go out on dates to nightclubs. I'm being introduced to partying and nightlife. I discover that I have an affinity to this life. The music, the dancing, the smell of liquor mixed with cigarette smoke, the tantalizing lights, and the rhythm of the music. It excites me to no end. We have a great deal of fun especially during the weekends. I frequently leave Jessica with my sisters while I go off partying with my new friend, Chad. He is introduced to my parents and sisters. Daddy and my sisters like him but of course mother dislikes him. He is not a member of her faith, but neither am I. At this point I simply want to enjoy life. Religion has no place in it. Six months into our relationship I become pregnant. This time I'm not devastated. I'm twenty years old and mature. I have my own place and am living my own life. Having another baby is not what I need but the inevitable has happened and I cannot change it. My mother notices the change in my stomach and asks if I'm pregnant. I tell her it's none of their business. Chad partially moves in with me, but he has the tendency to return to his mother with whom he still lives whenever we have a disagreement. He sleeps there two to three nights per week. I have no idea which night he'll be with me or when he chooses to go home to Mama. He's twenty-eight years old. This irritates me to no end, but I'm learning to deal with it.

The day I decide to tell him that I'm pregnant I call him at work verifying that he would be at my apartment that night. I plan a special romantic evening. Preparing his favorite meal accompanied by candlelight and music. Jessica is left to spend the night with my sisters.

Everything works according to plan. We enjoy a nice meal listen to music, dance together, later, retiring to bed.

"I have something to tell you." I say.

"Go ahead, I'm listening."

"I'm pregnant."

I'm a little apprehensive about what his reaction will be, but he quickly assures me that he is happy about the pregnancy and will be supportive. I'm relieved, but relief quickly turns to anger when he says that he also has something to tell me. My heart leaps. What is it? Is he married and had been keeping it a secret? Earlier in our relationship he told me that he had fathered a child when he was eighteen years old, and that his daughter lives with her mother in another part of the city.

"What do you have to tell me?" I asked.

"You are not going to like hearing this, but I have another child, a son, his name is Gregory. He is six years old and lives with his mother in Sunrise. I see him often, but his mother is now married and there is nothing between us."

This news hits me like a ton of bricks. It's better than if he had been married, but I'm still angry that he had kept this from me.
Angrily I ask. "Is there anything else I need to know about you while we're making confessions?"

"No Marcia, I have no secrets. There are no more skeletons in the closet."

"I don't want to be lied to. I'll be very upset if down the road I find out that you have been keeping things from me."

# The Odyssey of Survival

"I promise you my dear that there is nothing more in my life that I need to reveal to you. I love you and will be looking forward to the birth of our baby."

"I love you too."

Lying there in the dark listening to his steady breathing I reflect on the thought that he is the father of two children. I'm still mad that he had not told me before, but I have no right to be mad, after all I have not breathed one word of my sordid past to him. Except for the fact that I have a child, he knows nothing about me. The idea to tell him about my past crosses my mind, but the thought is quickly squashed, and remains locked away in the secret files of my mind. There are no upheavals in my life. Things remain on an even keel. We settle into a routine. By this time Bridget and Janice are in separate colleges, both pursing teaching careers. Bridget commutes to school, but Janice lives on campus, Cheryl, Anton, my nieces and my nephew are the only children in the home now. They are still ruled by an iron hand, but Mother doesn't dare sell Lynnette's daughters in the fashion she had sold her own. I speak to her only about the care of my child. She is not encouraged to visit me at my home. One Sunday morning uninvited and unannounced she shows up at my home. Ignoring me she marches through my front door and into my bedroom. Chad is asleep in bed, and she is shocked to see a man in my bed. She rushes out of the room while I stand there with a smirk on my face.

"Why didn't you tell me there was a man in your room?" she questioned.

"You did not ask. You simply walked into my bedroom without permission. What do you want?" I asked.

"To see my grandchild"

"As you can see she's asleep. Now I'm a big woman turning my own key in my own door. The next time you wish to make a visit to my home please call first."

# The Odyssey of Survival

"Don't worry I'll never set foot in this door again. This is exactly why I took Lynette's children from you because I don't know what kind of slackness you are carrying on around here."

"You have no reason to check up on Jessica; you'll see her tomorrow, you just wanted to pry into my business. Goodbye mama." In a huff she turns on her heels and walks away, never returning to my humble abode.

In my eighth month of pregnancy I ask Chad to reposition the furniture in the bedroom to make room for a bassinet for the new baby. He says he'll get around to it. I ask twice, getting the same answer.

"I'll get around to it."

It's Christmas time and I want it done now. But he has not gotten around to it yet. The New Year roars in and he still had not gotten around to it. So I decide to do it myself. In his absence I take on the task of moving Jessica's crib. I move the dresser and the other furniture around. While pushing and tugging the dresser I feel a sharp pain in my back, stopping what I'm doing sitting down on the bed. In a few minutes another pain this time of greater magnitude. I'm in trouble. The neighbors with cars have left for work, and there is no telephone in the apartment. My neighbor Stacy and her mother share an apartment next door. She also has a little girl who is Jessica's playmate. Thankfully they are home. Hobbling outside I knock on their door. It's opened and I tell them what's happening. I need to get to the hospital. Stacy runs to the street hailing a taxi, she jumps into the car accompanying me to my mother's home where I knew Janice was, still on Christmas vacation from school. Telling her what is going on; she yells the news to mother, then gets into the taxi with me. The ride to the hospital seems to be taking forever. It becomes evident that the baby was not going to wait. My sister begs the driver to drive faster. He tries but morning traffic on the street of Kingston is a nightmare. He tells me to hold on but matters are out of my control.

# The Odyssey of Survival

I cry out in pain, feeling the uncontrollable urge to push and knowing what it means. I say.

"The baby is coming."

"Try to hold on." I'm encouraged.

I try but to no avail. In the back seat of the taxi, with the poor driver frantic and with no medical help my baby is born. We don't know what to do. I know that my water had not broken but do not know the significance of that. My baby is born in a sac but none of us know what to do. We yell to the driver to hurry. Shortly after the birth we arrive at the hospital and the driver flies out of the car running to get help. They come running with a wheelchair. The nurse sizes up the situation rushing us into the emergency room yelling for a doctor to come at once. Immediately a medical team surrounds us. They cut the umbilical cord, rushing off with the baby. While the nurse is taking care of me I ask about the baby.

"How is my baby doing? We didn't know what to do, should we have broken the sac that he was in?"

"The doctors are working on him. We'll let you know his condition soon."

"Him, do I have a son?"

"Yes it's a boy. The doctor will talk to you as soon as he can."

I wait for the nurse to bring my son to me, just the way it had happened last time, but instead after about thirty minutes the doctor comes into my room grim faced. I know something is wrong. I look from one face to the other as the doctor begins speaking.

"We did our best to save your baby, but he spent too much time in the sac, he drowned in the fluid and to make matters worst, the umbilical cord was wrapped around his neck cutting off oxygen from his brain. Even if he had survived he would probably have suffered severe brain injury or be a vegetable. I'm sorry."

I cannot believe what I'm hearing. My baby is dead. Everything within me moves in agony and I begin retching, spewing vomit all over the bed. It was such a violent reaction that it takes the doctor by surprise. I scream and cry and they clean me up, changing the bed linen. The harsh reality is, I have lost my baby, and it is entirely my fault. The doctor ask if I would like to see him, and I tell him no. I know that I would not survive looking at his lifeless body, so I refuse to get a glimpse of my son. After some time Janice is allowed to visit me. She cries with me trying to console me. She had gotten a glimpse of him. She tells me how beautiful he was with a full head of black hair. But no amount of crying can bring him back to life; he is gone forever. Chad still has no idea that his baby has died. He had left for work and no one has thought of calling him. There had been no time to make the call.

Visiting hours are over and Janice leaves. I think it's a cruel thing to place a mother who has lost her baby in the same room with others whose babies are alive. As I listen to the mothers quietly talking to their babies, encouraging them to suck, comforting those who cry and hearing the happiness in their voices, I fall apart. I wail so loudly that the nurse, before giving me a sedative ordered by the doctor tells me that if I cry like this I will make myself sick. She also tells me that the only way to recover from the loss of a baby is to have another one as soon as possible. I don't want to hear anything about another child. I want my son. But no miracles could be performed. He is gone and I have to go on. The next day after the doctors visit their patients I'm told that although I had experienced such an awful loss, I have been released. The doctor said. "You are young and healthy and need healing of the spirit which we cannot provide. Go home and take care of yourself, sometimes things happen for the best even though they don't seem that way at first." I feel like smacking him in his face, instead I turn my face to the wall to hide my tears. Again there is no one waiting to take me home. I don't even know if my sisters had been able to contact Chad to tell him what had happened. I'm wheeled out

# The Odyssey of Survival

the front door, and just like two years earlier, the porter gets me a taxi, which takes me home. The difference is this time I return empty handed. Returning to the empty apartment is more than I can bear. A feeling of complete desolation sweeps over me. Throwing my head back I emitted a scream like none before, it fills the apartment, bringing my neighbors running. I am standing in the doorway, empty handed so they figure out what has happened and came to my aid. They hug and cry with me. Stacy helps me into bed, and stays for a while. Later that evening Chad comes home. For the first time he learns that his son has died. He sits down hard on the bed, covers his face with his hand and weeps.

"Why didn't someone tell me what happened. Why wasn't I called? You were in the hospital, the baby died two days ago and no one called me. Why?"

"It all happened so fast there was no time to call you. You know there are no telephones in the hospital rooms and I was released this morning. If you had come home last night you would have found out."

"Oh my God this is awful; I should have been there for you. I'm sorry you had to go through this alone. I promise to at least stop by every evening on my way home from work. I'm sorry I wasn't here, please forgive me. Oh my God, this is terrible."

"Are you all right?"

"No I am not alright, my baby just died. I feel like dying myself. I feel responsible for his death. I don't know how I'm going to survive this. Oh God help me."

In each other's arms we cry for what seems like an eternity, there we draw comfort from each other. We will have to get through this. My sisters bring Jessica home, and I hold her tightly pouring all my love into her. Three weeks later I return to work and everyone wants to know what happened. I tell them the story once. I tell them not to ask about it again because it's too difficult an experience to be related again. Taking pity on me they put the subject to rest, at least in my presence. Slowly I return to normal, I pretend to be all right but I'm not. The reel of events never stops playing in my mind. It doesn't matter what activity I'm engaged in, there is no stopping it. I cannot forgive myself and cry constantly for what I have done. If only I had not been so impatient. If only I had waited. If only… If I thought I was being tormented before, my own private hell has just begun. Now instead of dreaming of one lost child, I have two precious little souls looking for their mother. Don't ask me how, but in my dreams, my dead children have found each other. Hand in hand, two pairs of little feet patter around looking for their mom. Two distinct voices two babies crying for mommy. I am roaming through bushes, corridors, and rooms. Looking into cribs; under beds; under tables; in closets; into the faces of every child I pass, knowing I'll recognize mine. Looking everywhere for my children and hearing them yell, "Mommy, mommy." In unison both voices call out to me. "Where are you my babies, I'm trying to find you, I'm coming. I'll be right there."

My son was born and died on January 6$^{th}$ 1978. Two children have now been lost. I can either live in my grief or recover and live for the one I have. I decide that I will never forget my other two children, but the one who is alive needs me. I find a way to get on with my life, but always secretly mourning my losses, always crying for the children I have never held in my arms. No one shares in my private torment because I share them with no one.

# The Odyssey of Survival

"Then Job arose and rent his robe and shaved his head and fell down upon the ground and worshipped
And he said. Naked I came into this world from my mother's womb, and naked shall I depart. The Lord gave and the Lord has taken away, blessed be the name of the Lord."
Job 1: 20-21 (AKJV)

# The Odyssey of Survival

***Life question***: No one gets up in the morning and says "Today I'm going to do something stupid to ruin my life, or the life of someone else." Problems have their own way of creeping up on us, throwing us out in the deep blue ocean without a life jacket. Every time I hear about a woman who has ten children to feed, with the help of no father, or in some other improvised state. I quietly say. "But for the grace of God, there go I." My baby's death was caused by my own impatience, but I have learnt to console myself with the fact that God knows best. The longings will linger forever, the tears still come when the subject of lost children comes up, but I have released him into the hands of his creator, from whence he came. Is there a better way to deal with these types of losses? Has someone found a proven formula which you would like to share with the rest of us who have been struggling with the results of our past indiscretions, impatience, mistakes and failures? Is there life after loss?

***Answer:***

## Chapter Fourteen

## TWO NEW BABIES

At my parent's home one evening there is an abnormal, expectant hush in the air. Cheryl, our youngest sister seems petrified with a wild look in her eyes.

"What's going on?" I ask.

I'm escorted outside and in a hushed voice she tells me that she is pregnant and that the father of the baby is coming over to tell our parents.

"What, Oh my God, mama is going to kill you."

I am flabbergasted with the unexpected news. She is only fifteen, two years younger than I was when I got pregnant, and is a high school senior. I'm genuinely sorry for her.

"But it gets worst." she continues. "The father is one of my teachers from school."

O Lord, what is this? Now we're going to have two dead people. I'm going no place. This I have to see and hear. I linger talking with her, telling her that she can come to live with me if she wants to. That cheers her up a bit, but not for long as there is a knock at the gate. The brave young man has arrived. I quickly ask him if it's true and he confirms it. He also assures me that he is more than capable and willing to take full responsibility for his actions. He has no idea of what he is up against. I ask how and when this happened and he tells me how on several occasions he invited Cheryl to his home using the pretense of helping her with her homework. He had taken a great likeness to her and admits to taking advantage of her vulnerability. He is aware of the possibility of great trouble for him being an adult in a position of authority getting sexually involved with a minor. He is trying to be brave and is doing what he thinks to be the right thing.

Trouble looms large. Mother arrives home and is asking who and why there is a strange man in her home? None of us answers. He introduces himself plunging right in with both feet. Without missing a beat he tells her exactly who he is and why he's there. Anger is not an adequate description of her reaction. She vows to make him pay in more ways than he can even imagine for what he has done, then she kicks him out of the house. She turns on Cheryl.

"Another disgrace, another disappointment, another reason to hang my head in shame. None of you are any good. I sent you to school to learn how to spell your name so you wouldn't eat it on a bulla, not to sleep with your teacher. What the hell is wrong with the lot of you? Aren't any of you going to come out to be any good? I have only wasted my time and effort on all of you. I wish I had killed all of you at birth. Oh my God, I can't take any more of this. I can't go through this again. Find somewhere else to live and get out of my house. Get out of my sight."

I again offer my sister my home as a place of refuge, but mother overhears the conversation and refuses to allow her to leave the house. She doesn't want her there but will not let her leave. Within a few months her life becomes unbearable with the constant abuse. She tells the father of her baby about her home situation. He comes by with his car moving her out of the home placing her in his mother's home. We visit her there. She continues attending school until graduation. Dear mother has to get revenge. She reports the young man's conduct to the School Board and following an investigation into the charges he loses his job. He finds employment elsewhere but there is no hiding from her fury. Mother discovers where he works, reports him to his employers as a child molester and rapist, which ultimately leads to his dismissal. On my visit to the doctor for my postnatal exam I make a request for and am given oral contraception. The thought of getting pregnant again is not appealing. Being healthy and having never taken regular medication I have a hard time remembering to take the pills. Sometimes I miss days then I take two or more pills trying to make up for the missed doses I don't know what I'm doing. Only that I don't want to get pregnant again.

Sharon and her mother Peggy are my next-door neighbors. Peggy is an older woman who gives free and sometimes unwanted advice to the younger women in the apartment complex. She often relates stories about her life and some of her struggles raising her children without the help of her husband who left the family to form another family, forgetting about her and his six children. She has what we called in Jamaica a "goat's mouth." Meaning whatever she says almost always comes to pass. About two months after I lost my son, she looks at me with those narrowed piercing eyes, uttering deafening words.

"You are going to get pregnant very soon again."

"Not over my dead body."

"Whether your body is dead or alive you are going to get pregnant soon. Your body is ripe for a baby."

"What does that mean?" I ask her.

"When a woman loses a baby no matter what she does as long as she has a man in her bed she gets pregnant soon afterwards."

"I am taking the pill so that won't be true in my case."

"You can take all the pills you want. As long as that man you have in there is sleeping with you another baby will be on the way soon."

Laughing at her I dismiss her prediction as another of her old wives tales. I share her prediction with Chad. He sums it up.

## The Odyssey of Survival

"Whatever will be will be." No one knows the future. If it happens we'll deal with it."

We certainly do not know the future and Peggy does have a goat's mouth. Because two months later I discover that I'm pregnant again. I'm not excited. I think it's too soon after the loss and I become concerned about my body's ability to properly sustain another baby so soon. I had given birth to my son in January and this is only April, too soon to go through another pregnancy. But regardless of what I think another baby had been conceived and its life has to be sustained.

Chad's family and I have grown close. His mother is a lovely lady and his brothers and sisters are great people. Three of the adult sons still live at home, including Chad, who still sleeps there whenever he feels like it. I tell their mother she has spoiled them. She agrees but does not encourage them to leave and fend for themselves. With this second pregnancy Chad and I begin talking about getting married. I want to and would love to marry him but I'm having concerns about him being so tied to his mother's apron string. I decide to talk to his mother about my concerns. Visiting her on a Sunday afternoon; over cool drinks I tell her about the new pregnancy and about the step we are thinking about taking. She smiles at me, tells me how much she likes me and that she thinks I am a wonderful young lady who would make a good wife, but that I should not waste my time marrying Chad.

"I am pregnant again and he says he is tired of living like a bachelor. He agrees that we should provide a stable home for the children."

"My dear, Chad is just like his father who left me with nine children to care for on my own. Of all the boys he is most like him. See how often he leaves you alone and comes here at night? That's exactly what he'll do even when you are married. He doesn't like responsibilities and I'm sorry to tell you, but if you marry him he won't change. His father was the same way until one day he left and never came back. I suggest you have the baby, he'll support both of you, but if you try to tie him down with marriage he'll run."

# The Odyssey of Survival

I'm crushed, but it is true. He always leaves our place at the slightest hint of a disagreement, staying away for days before returning, but I think he will change his ways once we become husband and wife. His mother has dashed these hopes, and for once in my life I decide to listen to someone who knows what she's talking about. I can't help being pregnant, but I can stop myself from being stuck in an unhappy marriage. I know what it feels like to be in an unhappy home. If at any time he wants his freedom, I will not stand in his way.

That night I tell Chad that we need more time to get to know each other better. If after the baby's birth he still feels the same way, we would get married then. With almost a sigh of relief he agrees. I'm thankful to his mother for giving me an honest answer regarding her son. He is fun to be with, but he does not portray the ability to provide the stability that I'm looking for and need. When the party is over and reality stares us in the face he does not seem to have the gumption to square his shoulders and take on whatever life brings his way. Instead he retreats to Mama's house and goes to sleep. We have a baby to prepare for and right now my most important task is to take care of myself, and protect both of my children, born and unborn. Chad is not as good a provider as I hoped he would be. He makes a good salary but continues partying and hanging out with his friends at night, spending too much money on the street instead of in his home. I'm pretty much responsible for making all the preparations for the baby. He hates confrontations making it almost impossible for us to have serious conversations or make long-term plans. Jessica and I spend many Sunday afternoons at his mother's home. She welcomes us whether he is there or not. I became attached to her finding in her what my own mother lacks. During one of our frequent conversations about the sex of the baby Chad expresses his desire for a son. I want another daughter. I can envision an angelic face with masses of black curly hair, just like her dad's. I dream of how beautiful a child between us will be and cannot envision having to cut off those beautiful curls instead of allowing them to hang down the little girl's back.

# The Odyssey of Survival

I talk to her, sing to her, assuring her that regardless of what happens it will be me, she and Jessica against the world.

My pregnancy so soon after my loss surprises everyone, my godfather comments on it and I simply ignore his comments. I stay away from my parent's home, instead asking my sisters to bring Jessica home in the evenings for me. My mother's opinion of the obvious is of no interest to me. The path my life is heading down is not ideal but I'm struggling to come to terms with everything that has happened; desperately trying to find myself.

I'm twenty-one years old and pregnant for the fourth time. My first child is three years old, the second one had been aborted without my consent, and the third one died, the fourth will be born in the same year. This may seem like promiscuous behavior to most people, but I'm not living an irresponsible life style. Unfortunate events have happened and pregnancies are the result of some of these events. The enormity of the situation is not lost on me, and now that I am more mature and have the life long responsibility of caring for these innocent children, definite changes will be made in my life. After the birth of this baby the use of some type of reliable contraceptive will be practiced and if Chad and I do not get married I will not bring another child into the world under these circumstances.

Cheryl is almost at her due date. Mother wants her home so she can have more control over her life, beating her into the ground, breaking her spirit. Her baby's father refuses to bring her back. That does not deter mother. She makes such a stink at his mother's home that Cheryl is encouraged to pack her bags and leave with her mother. On September 4th, 1976, Cheryl gives birth to a beautiful baby girl. The father is present at the hospital for his daughter's birth. Mother makes his life miserable, but he sticks to his word and does not abandon his child. The beautiful baby girl is named Nadine Denise Roseanne. She is beautiful, as precious as the most priceless jewels of the queen of Sheba. We love her.

## The Odyssey of Survival

December arrives and I'm in the eight month of my pregnancy. I decide to continue working until the end of the year. Friday the 29$^{th}$ will be my last day. At the end of an exhausting day I go home, planning to return on Saturday to clean off my desk, put files in order and be off on three months maternity leave. My baby's due date is early January of the following year.

On my doctor's advice, we made arrangements for a midwife who lives nearby to deliver my baby at home. He's concerned that I may have a repeat of the last episode because of the distance from the hospital. We have had a couple meetings with this lovely lady. She gave us instructions of how to prepare for the birth once I'm in labor. I share her instructions with my sisters, whom I hope will be around to provide the support I need.

Very tired after a long day at work, I lay down to rest, shortly after I'm forced out of bed by hunger pangs. Cooking is not on the agenda. So Sharon and I walk over to a restaurant to purchase a bowl of soup. Back in my apartment Sharon brings me a slice of hot potato pudding, straight from the oven. It is washed down by a bottle of cold cream soda… "hmm delicious". Almost immediately there is a burning in my stomach. Heartburn, I ate that piece of pudding too fast. Two antacids go down the hatch. The heartburn persists, and I go to bed. My sisters bring Jessica home; and find me reclining in bed. What's wrong? They ask. "I have such a bad heartburn."

"What did you eat?" They have often chided me about my poor diet.

"I had a bowl of soup, a slice of potato pudding, and a bottle of soda." "And you wonder why you have heartburn?"

Without warning, a contraction rips through my body. I gasp for air, grabbing my stomach. A second contraction follows with more intensity. I am in labor. My sister and niece hurry to get Miss Price the midwife, while between contractions I tell Bridget and Alicia to boil a pot of water, gather several towels and plastic bags. Taking a shower means hanging on to the walls as contractions rip through me. I hope Chad comes home soon. The contractions are coming so quickly together that I begin to fear the baby will get here before Miss Price does. She gets here not a minute too soon. She assesses the situation, puts on her gloves and gown giving quick instructions to my sisters. Behind the closed bedroom door, with six pairs of twitching ears glued to the door they listen to hear me scream.

I bite my lip until it bleeds, grinding my teeth together. I push hard and do what I have to do. But not one scream escapes my throat. After only four hours of labor, at 11:45 pm, Friday December 29th 1978, my second daughter enters the world, clearing her lungs with her first cry. Miss Price changes the sheets and gathers the used items. She makes me comfortable and places my daughter in my arms. What an angel. That's the only way to describe her. A perfect little angel has descended from heaven blessing me with her presence. All six and one quarter pounds, twenty inches of her are every mother's dream. Her perfectly formed head and face glows with life. Her full head of black hair is like running your fingers through silken threads. Her features are as if formed by the very hands of God himself as he lovingly shaped her forehead, straightened her nostrils, kissed her lips and set her jaw at just the right angle. Her fingers lovingly curl around my finger as I kiss each one. She is gorgeous and I love the beautiful sight, savoring the delicious smell of her, I hold her close to my heart.

    Miss Price completes her work and opens the door. My sisters are all standing there waiting for news of us. The room has been quiet, except for the sound of a crying newborn infant. They come in full of excitement.

    "How come we didn't hear anything? We thought you would be screaming. Didn't it hurt? O my goodness; look at her. She is beautiful."

    She is gorgeous. In hushed voices they exclaim at her beauty. Very carefully she is placed in the arms of her big sister Jessica who thinks she has just been given a new doll. Nicole Amanda nicknamed

# The Odyssey of Survival

Nia. She takes a firm hold on the hearts of her family. Her daddy has no idea that his daughter has been born. We still have no telephone; he will just have to wait until he shows up to partake in her essence. Placing her on my chest I begin singing to her. I know I'm off key, but she doesn't care. One of my sisters spends the night with us. I drift off into sleep.

Saturday morning dawns bright and beautiful. As the neighbors awake and news of the late arrival is made known, other neighbors visit to wish us well, each bringing a covered dish. They stop by to catch a glimpse of the little one. I proudly show her off even as she peacefully sleeps. Chad shows up Saturday afternoon almost falling over when he realizes what has happened. He is disappointed that he missed her birth. I try hard not to say it serves you right. He is in awe of her, holding her for hours; even while she sleeps.

I begin noticing that when she is touched a yellow tint is left on her. Her eyes are not as clear as they should be. I'm concerned, but the midwife will be visiting in two days. So I wait. Miss Price shows up for a visit and makes sure I am doing well. I explain my concern about the yellowing of Nia's skin. She tells me that the blood, which had been drawn at birth, had been tested and the results revealed that my baby is seriously jaundiced. "What does this mean? Is she going to be all right?"

Miss Price gently tells me that if Nia had been born in the hospital she would have been placed under an ultra violet lamp for hours to decrease the Bill Rubin in her blood; she now needs to be placed under this light daily to avoid liver damage. How can I do this? I do not drive and I'm not sure if Chad will be able to take the time necessary. The only other alternative is for me to sit in the morning sun holding her for about four hours each morning. I have to be careful to protect her eyes from the direct sunlight. For one month I sit outside with my baby across my lap, exposing one section of her for a few minutes, turning her over at intervals to prevent burning her skin.

# The Odyssey of Survival

Slowly her skin tone improves and her yellowed eyes become as clear as crystal. Through all this discomfort she was still a very happy child, crying rarely.

Another problem raises its ugly head. Her belly button protrudes, forming into a large object, growing right along with her. The doctors examine the protrusion, shaking their heads commenting that they have never seen such a large umbilical hernia. One specialist suggests surgery but is quick to tell me that one has never been performed on a child under the age of five years old. But he is concerned with the rapid growth of Nia's stomach distension. He explains that the cavity in the navel is a serious problem. Her intestines have the potential to become entangled causing an even greater problem. Nia has been experiencing trouble with digestion, a direct result of her umbilical hernia.

At the time of Nia's birth, Cheryl's daughter Nadine is three months old. Nadine has a difficult time attaching herself to her mother's breast and refuses to take the bottle. We are concerned about her nutrition and I suggest trying to feed her. On the very first attempt she grasped my breast with her lips hanging on for dear life. She sucks until she is full. From that day and for the next six months I become her mother. I breastfeed both babies as if they were twins, sometimes feeding them at the same time. All three children are growing up as sisters.

At six weeks Nia and I make a scheduled visit to the pediatrician's and my OB/GYN's office. Nia's blood test reveals that her jaundice is under control but her stomach cavity is weak. Her umbilical hernia has been getting progressively worse. Surgery will be necessary as soon as she is old enough. During the visit to my gynecologist I adamantly tell him that I want a permanent form of contraception. Tubal Ligation, he tells me is the most effective contractive, with a 99% success rate. When can I have it done?

# The Odyssey of Survival

He refuses to perform the procedure, citing that I am young and unmarried; therefore I do not make a good patient for such a permanent procedure. Instead he educates me on the reliability of the IUD and I gladly agreed and have the device inserted into my uterus.

Nia's recovery from jaundice does not last. She needs more than sunlight. In a couple months, her skin turns bright yellow and she becomes very ill. We take her to the hospital where she is admitted. The ultra violet treatment is not as successful as hoped. The doctor decides that she needs a blood transfusion to save her from permanent liver damage. Her father's blood is tested and found to be suitable. We spend tense hours in the hospital waiting room until we are finally able to hold our baby in our arms again. We hope that she is going to be all right.

Before receiving the transfusion Nia's illness is constant. We are always at the doctor's office or hospital emergency room for one ailment or another. She is truly a beautiful child, a pleasure to have around. Through all her illnesses, her personality remains cheerful which prompts another observation from my neighbor, Peggy. We had just come in from sitting out in the sun one morning, when Peggy took a look at us, remarking.

"That child is not going to live. She is too pretty. Those pretty babies usually don't live"

I am furious. How could she say such a thing to me after she had so recently witnessed the loss of my son? Fuming I face her.

"She is going to live; if I have to give my life to her she is going to live. Whatever I have to do, she will live. You're an awful person for saying such a thing about a baby. She will live. You'll see." I hug my baby tightly to my chest, I cry at the pronouncement that has been made on her life and I pray.

"Please God take care of my baby, please make her live."

# The Odyssey of Survival

She lives. Thank God, but her young life is full of constant illnesses, and surgeries. She recovers from her jaundice, but another problem arises. We notice the constant pulling on her ear lobe, and when her temperature spikes to 104 degrees, we rush her to the doctor's office. She has an inner ear infection. This becomes chronic; tubes are inserted into her ears. It is amazing how one child can be so healthy and the other so plagued with illnesses. The appearance of large tumors on her buttocks surprises us. And off to the hospital we go. The doctors diagnose an allergic reaction to Milo. They keep appearing all over her body, necessitating many trips to the hospital to have them surgically removed. Each tumor leaves an indentation on her body. She will have many reminders of her childhood illnesses.

Watching Nia crawl is pitiful. Her distended hernia is of such magnitude that she appears to have three legs. This huge growth drags along behind her on the floor as she makes her way around the apartment. When she stands erect, the hernia looks like an elephant's trunk; it also distorts her little body. It's difficult to securely fasten her diapers and her clothes do not fit properly. She is under the constant supervision of specialists who shake their heads, as they discuss the rapid growth of her hernia.

Nia turns fifteen months; her doctors call us in for a conference with a specialist. They are very concerned with the growth of the hernia. They tell us that although they have never performed this surgery on a child under the age of five years, our baby's condition warrants it. They are worried that her intestines were becoming entangled causing more problems. We know she has digestive problems. The medical team proposes performing the surgery in three months, when she will be a year and a half. With great apprehension we discuss this turn of events, agreeing to allow the surgery. We take our baby home fussing over her showering her with love. We wish she could be spared until she is older, but her condition needs to be rectified now.

On the morning of the surgery we awake to torrential rain as though the angels are weeping for this little one who is about to endure

# The Odyssey of Survival

her ordeal. Chad and I bundle her up, and off we go to the hospital. The nurses prepare her for surgery. An intravenous needle is placed in her little arm. They draw her blood and record her vitals. We had been instructed to withhold food from the previous evening so she is hungry, but we cannot feed her. The doctor speaks with us, and then our baby is wheeled away to surgery. I am almost paralyzed with fear. The surgeon told us that general anesthetic would be administered to her. The rain suits our mood. Today is the hardest day Chad and I have experienced as parents. Hours pass with us knowing nothing about her condition. We notice that all the other parents who were waiting for children in surgery have been called to their children's side, except for us, who gloomily sit there holding hands, waiting for words about our precious Nia.

A lifetime later a nurse approaches us, asking us to follow her. We are led to the recovery room, there we're told that our baby has experienced an adverse reaction to the anesthetic and they are having problems reviving her. The nurse instructs me to try to wake her up. My heart is heavy with fear. What had happened to her? She appears to be in a deep sleep. Reaching down into the bed I pat her back, together we stroke her head, brushing her cheeks. We call her name; I pick her up holding her in my arms, rocking and calling her name. But she sleeps on. She is breathing ever so softly; the nurse brings us a chair. I sit down rocking and bouncing my baby on my knees. We take turns doing as much as possible to make her open her eyes. An hour later her eyes flutter. With glazed pupils she looks around trying to catch a glimpse of something or someone familiar. Our hearts soar with joy. She is alive, we hold her close to our bosoms, kissing her. Her vitals are checked, and I'm given a small amount of glucose to feed her. She is hungry crying for more. Crying could loosen the stitches in her abdomen. That's one of the reasons this surgery is usually not done prior to age five. Babies cry. She needs to remain in the hospital overnight, and her release depends on how well she recovers. She is transferred to a room and I have every intention of spending the night by her side, but the nurses insist that we leave. I beg them to allow me to spend the night with her but they refuse. Reluctantly we kiss her leaving her in a cold hospital room.

## The Odyssey of Survival

Two days later we take her home with special instructions. She should not be allowed to cry. The incision needs to heal. Crying will prolong the process. The area has to be cleaned and dressed daily. My queasy stomach barely allows me to perform this task, but it needs to be done. For the next two weeks we watch her with eagle eyes. Our weekly doctor's visits confirm that she is making good progress. Two weeks later I have to accompany my godfather to Miami for consultation to remove cataracts from his eyes. His failing vision makes it difficult for him to travel alone so the job falls on my shoulders. We'll be there for five days. Since Nia is recovering well, I think it will be okay for me to go. My children are left in the care of my parents and sisters. I am thrilled at the prospect of flying and leaving Jamaica for the first time. No one knows that I'm scared of flying. As the airplane taxis down the runway, the butterflies in my stomach almost stifle me. My knuckles are white, as I hold on tightly to the armrest. The special treatment reserved for heads of government is lavished on us. We are met by important people and promptly cleared through customs security. A chauffeur meets us and we are escorted to a Rolls Royce. I wish my family could get a glimpse of me as I settle into its luxurious leather. Accommodations in Florida are at a posh beachfront home in Boca Raton. The lavishness of the residence makes my eyes round. The beach is a few feet away from the deck to which an unbelievable yacht is anchored. It sparkles as the sunlight dances off the water inviting one to come on in. I fall in love with Florida deciding then and there that one day I will live here. The time between doctor's appointments is spent cruising on the yacht, visiting friends and being entertained in all manner of ways. I get a good preview into the lives of the rich and famous.

The cataract surgery is set for two months away. I shop for my family and children, returning home with a suitcase filled with clothes and toys for the children. In my absence Jessica and Nia missed me but their eyes are round with joy when they open all the new toys from America. During my absence, my baby's stitches came apart. My return home was not one day too soon. Nia's stomach is a gaping hole with her intestines almost spilling out of the cavity. I spend the night holding her in my arms. Her temperature is 104 degrees. I call Chad

## The Odyssey of Survival

telling him of our baby's condition. My mother, while never missing an opportunity to get into everyone's life and business had neglected to call him so he could have taken her to the hospital. He on the other hand thought that since Nia was with my mother she was being cared for and had not visited the children while I was out of the country. I'm too concerned about my baby to get mad at either one of them right then. I just pray that she will make it through the night.

At the hospital the following morning she is admitted. The incision has to be sutured and her temperature brought under control. Two days later they feel she is well enough to return home. Every day for ten days she has to be taken to the hospital to have her wound cleaned and dressed.

With tender loving care her body heals but not without leaving an awful folding of skin and scars where a neat belly button should have been. She will never be able to wear a bikini to the beach.

Eight weeks later I again accompany my godfather to Florida to undergo cataract surgery. We are met at the airport by the same chauffeured driver's Rolls Royce and driven to the beachfront property in Boca Raton; we remain here for the two days prior to the surgery. Two days later we are driven to Miami and booked into the Omni Hotel. On the evening before the surgery I leave him upstairs, take the elevator downstairs to the mall hoping to explore and do some shopping. Strolling along, browsing through the stores I'm oblivious to the fact that I am being watched. A young man approaches me. With a smile on his face he greets me.

"Hi pretty lady."

"Hello."

"You from yard?"

"Yes. I'm from Jamaica."

"It so good to meet someone from yard. You live here?"
"No, just visiting."

"You are the right person mi want to meet, a yardie. Come here mi want to share something with you. You can't trust everybody but since we are the same mi going to share this with you."

I'm led to a bench and he sits down next to me. He opens the top of the brown paper bag giving me a glimpse of its contents. In a hushed voice he explains. "I just came into this unexpected fortune. I have thousands of dollars in here and have been looking for someone to share it with. Mi just found the right person. Mi know things hard back home so mi want to share it with you."

"Why would you do that?"

"Because mi want to help a yardi. This is how it works. You must promise not to tell anyone about this and the only way mi can trust you to do that since mi don't know you is for you to give me one hundred dollars."

"Why would I give you $100? I don't know you."

"Well when you give me $100, I give you $5000. You lose nothing. Your up front money is just telling me that you deserve this good fortune."

The reasoning sounds good to me. I pull out my purse, produce the only money I have, a $100 bill and hand it over to him.

"Ok. Mi don't want all these people to see me counting out all this money so let me go separate your share and bring it back to you. Stay right here, I'll be right back."

"Ok. I hope I can trust you."

"Watch the time. I'll be back in exactly ten minutes."

## The Odyssey of Survival

Two hours later I'm still sitting in the same spot, waiting for him to return with my money. Eventually it dawns on me that I had been taken for a ride. I feel like a big fool. Angry tears sting my eyes. Looking around to see if anyone had witnessed my stupidity I see a salesman who had wished me a good day looking at me from the doorway. Our eyes meet and he ever so slightly shakes his head, purses his lips and retreats into the store. He had just witnessed another unsuspecting victim to a crime. I feel sick to my stomach and want to cry. I just lost all the money I had to shop. What am I going to tell my children who are looking for gifts? With slumped shoulders I take the elevator back upstairs Uncle Duke hears me coming in the door, and asks.

"How was your shopping?"

"I'll go back tomorrow, just wanted to see what was available downstairs." I replied.

"Beware that you do not despise or feel scornful toward or think little of one of these little ones, for I tell you that in heaven their angels always are in the presence of and look upon the face of My Father who is in heaven.
For the son of man came to save that which was lost."
Matthew 18: 10-11

# The Odyssey of Survival

**Life Question:** *No one knows the trouble that we bear. No one knows the longings and loneliness of our heart. Those who have suffered loss only know the pain of losses. What is it within us that keeps us going even when our lives or everything around us is telling us to lie down and never get up again. Would you have done anything differently if you were faced with these same set of circumstances?*

**Answer:**

## *Chapter Fifteen*

## FREEDOM – FROM MOTHER

It is time for Lynnette's children to migrate to Canada. They will be missed, but they need their mother. As the day of their departure approaches we spend as much time as possible with them, knowing that when they leave we have no idea when we we'll see them again. We seem to be losing our family to Canada. The country has now claimed eleven of my family members. My parents' house is strangely quiet without my nieces and nephew; I dream of the day when I too will leave the shores of Jamaica for a brighter future. Working for my godfather continues. His raping has stopped since the St. Thomas episode. My life is beginning to take on some form of normalcy; I still harbor great resentment towards him. Going to work daily is a chore, but it has its benefits. I don't have to struggle on the bus to get to work, when I need to take care of my children's illnesses, it is never a problem and If Chad is unavailable to take us to the doctor or hospital, the chauffeured car is always available.

Janice has completed college and is employed at a private school at Jamaica House. Children of the country's dignitaries almost exclusively attend this school. She enrolls Jessica there and takes her with her in the mornings. I am very grateful to her. Tuition is quite expensive but my daughter attends for free. She is receiving a good basic education and plays with the children of the crème de la crème; all for free. Mother continues caring for Nia during the day.

Lester introduces an attractive young lady named Kelly to the family. They have been living together. Mother hates her, swearing to do everything in her power to break them up. Kelly falls in love with Jessica on their first meeting. She begins expressing a desire for a little girl just like her. Her love for my child becomes an obsession causing us to carefully watch her every movement on her frequent visits. Six months later she gleefully announces her pregnancy with what she hopes will be a little girl. As the pregnancy progresses she becomes very ill. Her morning sickness is almost debilitating, and instead of gaining weight she begins losing it. Her doctor becomes concerned and run tests. To everyone's dismay she is diagnosed with leukemia. Lester is devastated, and Kelly is terrified. What will be the outcome of the pregnancy? Mother is convinced that God is punishing Kelly for what she calls her insolence. She has been one of the few people who is not intimidated by mother; instead she stands up to her unreasonable demands, defending herself against the verbal abuse and lies she tells Lester about her. Returning home with the smugness of a cat that had gotten the cream, mother proudly recounts her latest encounter with Kelly. She showed up at their apartment unannounced. Without knocking she walks in the unlocked door, which Kelly leaves that way in case of emergencies. Following sounds she finds Kelly huddled on the bathroom floor, hugging the commode. Kelly is relieved that someone has come to help her. She stretches up her hand begging to be helped up from the floor. Mother laughs in the face of the one prostrate before her, telling her that God has finally avenged her for all the times she had been rude to her. She tells her that seeing her in that position, helpless and begging is the best revenge she could have asked for. Mother then turns on her heels leaving on the bathroom floor the mother of her son's unborn child, a woman who is dying from cancer.

    A couple weeks later she is hospitalized. She has been unable to digest food to sustain herself and her growing baby. The doctors prescribe complete bed rest and a special diet. The special diet and bed rest achieves nothing. She continues experiencing violent episodes of illnesses. In the fifth month of her pregnancy she is hospitalized again. She will remain there until she gives birth. Her prognosis is terminal. All they can do for her now is keep her hospitalized to give the baby a fighting chance. She is expected to die as soon as she delivers her baby.

# The Odyssey of Survival

Lester is inconsolable. We pray and hope for a change in the prognosis. None comes. During the seventh month it's clear that her demise is imminent. The vivacious young lady, whom we have come to know and love, who has fallen head over heels in love with my daughter, has been reduced to a skeleton. Bare bones with a small lump of a stomach, is the only proof that a life is clinging on inside of her, it's the only indication of what is to be. She barely recognizes us, as she exists between reality and a drug-induced stupor. Hugging the skeletal frame almost lost within the folds of white sheets, it is painfully apparent that this is the last time we will see her. Lester regrets the pregnancy, believing that if she had not gotten pregnant she would at least have had a fighting chance at survival.

The following day Lester gives us the sad news that the baby had been delivered by caesarian section, but Kelly had lost her fight with leukemia. One life had come into the world at the expense of another. Lester has gained a daughter, but has lost the love of his life. With members of both families at his side Lester buries Kelly. Then he takes home his baby daughter, whom he names Crystal. He is heart broken, but there is little time to lie down and grieve. Crystal has to be cared for. A side effect of the immense amount of drugs administered to her mother, Crystal suffers health problems of her own. She appears to be a little slow in her mental development. She walks late, talks late; she potty- trains late and displays problems with retention of simple instructions. She has trouble with basic aptitude and memorizing the alphabet. Concerned for her future, and worried that the programs to help Crystal develop into a high functioning young lady will not be available either from Lester or from the Jamaican Government, Amelia decides to file a petition with Canadian Immigration allowing her to adopt and sponsor the child into Canada. Lester agrees to this proposal. With the help of an attorney little Crystal is granted permission to join her new adopted mother in Canada, where the necessary medical treatment is both available and affordable.

# The Odyssey of Survival

Mother is invited to accompany four-year-old Crystal on the trip to Canada. Mother is also invited to remain in Canada with Amelia for an extended period. She accepts the invitation. The idea that she will be out of our lives even for a short time is exhilarating. The years have done nothing to mellow her into a nice person. We have matured to the point where she has been unable to exert total control over our lives, but she is still a force to be reckoned with. Daddy tried his best to remain at home but had not been able to. One morning in a fit of rage she threw his beloved keyboard along with all his belongings out the door, kicking him out right behind them. Daddy, after raising all these children has found himself alone, in a rented room, fending for himself. Her impending departure is good news. She will not be missed.

Conversation with mother has been limited to the affairs of my children. I am surprised, when she asks to speak with me one evening, as I gather my daughters to take them home. Curiosity gets the better of me, and I sit down to listen.

"You know that Amelia has adopted Crystal and she will be going to Canada to live with her?"

"Yes I know. That was nice of Amelia because Crystal is going to need care, and there is none here to care for her properly."

"Yes, but more than that she has asked me to bring up Crystal and remain there with her for a vacation."

"That's a good thing. You need a vacation. How long will you be gone?"

"That's why I need to talk to you. My visa is for five years and Amelia says I can stay for about two years, come back for a few months and return again."

"That sounds good."

# The Odyssey of Survival

"It sounds good, but I can't just leave Cheryl in the house with Anton. Janice and Bridget are here, but they are all still young. So I have been wondering if you would be willing to move back in here to take care of the children and provide adult supervision while I'm gone."

 I'm flabbergasted. She has actually invited me back into her home and even called me an adult. I listen to the proposal, and promise to discuss it with Chad. I relate the story to my sisters and they love the idea. The prospect of all of us living together again is exciting. Chad is not crazy about the idea of my giving up the apartment and moving back into my parent's home, we won't be able to continue living together under the new arrangements. He allows me to make my own decision. Although I enjoy being with him the prospect of a long-term relationship culminating in marriage is still uncertain. After lengthy discussions I accept the offer to move back home. Chad returns to his mama. And my brother, Leroy, decides to take over the apartment.

To the airport we go carrying mother and Crystal to board their flight to Canada. From the gallery we wave goodbye. The anticipation of a home without her is overwhelming. Around us on the waving gallery others are crying for their loved ones, they must think we are crazy because we are all smiles and laughter. For the first time in all of our lives, we are free from Mother's wrath. Not a tear is shed at her departure. We return home from the airport and throw the first party ever held in the home. We talk and laugh freely staying up late watching television. We are free from her iron hand. Living on my own with my two children has had its hardships. After paying the mortgage, utilities and food, very little is left for anything else. Uncle Duke is wealthy, but I ask for nothing, in his opinion I am being paid a good salary, so I leave it at that. My sisters often assist with groceries and Janice takes great pleasure in shopping for her nieces. They are the most beautiful and best-dressed little girls in the community.

Returning home is the beginning of the end of the relationship between Chad and me. Over time he visits less frequently, until now he sees the children only when I take them to visit him at his mother's home. By this time Jessica's father has gotten married. He had asked for my hand in marriage three times, always-receiving no for an answer. He has moved on with his life, leaving his daughter behind. He's providing no financial support, and we fare no better with Chad. I'm raising my children on my own. But life isn't hard. Three of us work, so with our pooled resources the benefits of working for one common goal is easier.

My girls are five and two years old. Janice is now teaching at a High School, and Jessica has been registered in Holy Childhood Preparatory School, a private school costing more than I can afford per term. Providing a solid education for my children is very important to me; so making the sacrifice is well worth the effort. Nia and Nadine are in kindergarten together. My girls enjoy living in a household of aunts, uncles, and cousins; there are no shortage of hands to hold, arms to hug and cheeks to kiss. They lack nothing. We lavish so much on them they become just a little pampered. Jessica receives a cute puppy from a friend. We name him Bruno. The puppy grows into a huge German shepherd, jumping over chairs and knocking the girls off their feet. We love Bruno but Jessica is petrified of him due to his sheer size. One Sunday evening I take the girls to visit Chad' mother. Nia is playing inside; while Jessica explores the front yard. Out of nowhere a dog appears. Jessica catches a glimpse of him and begins running into the house. The dog, sensing her fear lunges at her, grabbing hold of her dress as she dashes for the door. Her screams bring us running outside. Attached to the hem of her dress is a dog; refusing to let go. We run to help her. The sight and the look of terror on her face are frightening. Grabbing a broom, I beat the dog until he releases my daughter. This episode has done nothing to alleviate Jessica's fear of dogs. She is frightened of them. By the time the dog loosens his grip on her dress she is practically naked. He has torn the dress off from the waist. There is no consoling her, so we go home. This ends the visits to Chad's mother. Jessica refuses to return.

Bridget is teaching at our alma mater. She becomes pregnant. After a difficult pregnancy she has a caesarian delivery of a baby boy named Andrew. He is a quiet child growing into a very intelligent boy.

# The Odyssey of Survival

He loves his mother above all others. Bridget is known for her lack of culinary skills but Andrew bravely eats whatever she prepares. Even when everyone knows the meal tastes disgusting he chews, wincing in agony, swallowing each offending morsel. But he always thanks his mom for a delicious meal. He is a sweetheart.

Uncle Duke has to pay another visit to Florida. Again I'm his designated traveling companion. We will be leaving on Monday. Sunday afternoon I'm walking home from visiting a friend. A car slows down as it approaches me. Slowing my steps I look at the unfamiliar driver. The car stops next to me and the driver leans out to speak to me. Ahh, I know who it is, it's the owner of a farmers' market where I do my weekly shopping. He introduces himself.

"Hi. Thought it was you. Can I give you a ride to where you are going?"

"Hi there, thanks, but I'm almost home."

"Do you live around here?"

"Yes. Do you?"

"No I'm taking a short cut through here to Pembroke Hall where I live." He says as he extends his hand.

"By the way my name is Norris O'Connor. You come into the store every week but I have no idea who you are. What's your name pretty lady?"

"I'm Marcia."

"Hello Marcia. I must tell you that you are a beautiful lady. I like you and have been waiting for an opportunity to ask you out. Are you married?"

"Thank you, no I'm not married."

"Good. Can I take you out for dinner and a little dancing tonight?"

"I would love to go but I'm leaving for Florida early tomorrow morning and need to pack."

"Oh man, just my luck. After all this time as soon as I get to talk to you, you are leaving for America."

"I'll only be gone for ten days."

"That's what you say, no one who goes to America ever comes back, so I guess its hello and goodbye."

"Not me. This is my third visit to Florida. I'll be back and as soon as I return I'll come to the store."

"Promise?"

"I promise. Take care."

The trip to Florida is without incident, business is accomplished and we return home to resume life as normal. A few days later I visit the farmers market to purchase supplies and Norris is immediately at my side. He tells me how glad he is to see me, confessing he had doubts that I would have returned from the USA. "I have no intention of leaving Jamaica, at least not yet."

The following Friday I'm back in the store. Norris' face lightens up when he sees me. We talk for a while exchanging telephone numbers. Later that night, he calls me inviting me to dinner and a movie on Saturday night. I refuse the offer, telling him I didn't know him and do not trust strangers. On Sunday he calls again, asking for an invitation to my home so we can talk, and get to know each other. I give him my address and he shows up. He meets the family. We talk for about two hours. As the following weekend approaches, he invites me to a barbeque at his cousin's home in Red Hills.

# The Odyssey of Survival

He promises to return me safely. I accept the invitation. We enjoyed the evening. Driving home he suggests stopping at a nightclub.

"My favorite club is right down the street, it's owned by a friend of mine. Do you mind if we stop for a drink?"

"I don't want to go to a club, can you just take me home."

"Come on, don't be a spoiled sport. We had a good afternoon let's finish it off with a drink."

"Okay, but not for too long; I want to go home."

"I promise not to keep you out too late. I don't want to make you mad at me and not go out with me again. We'll only stay one hour."

Before long he has me on the dance floor pleading for just one dance. We dance to one song, two songs then to three. Before long its two hours. Glancing at the time I become adamant about going home. He reluctantly obliges. At the door I'm met by one of my sisters telling me that I'm in trouble.

"What have I done to be in trouble?"

"Chad came by to take you out. Daddy, who was visiting us for the day, told him you were out on a date. He got upset and left in a huff."

It has been months since he showed any interest in either Nia or me. Tough luck, if his feathers have been ruffled. I no longer care. With mother in Canada, Daddy moved back home. It's good having him back. Soon Norris and I are going out weekly. On Friday evenings as soon as he closes his business, he comes right over to my home. Frequently, in the back of his car is a box; laden with meat, vegetables, fruits, and other items from his store, and always hidden somewhere in the box are treats for the three girls. Often he takes them to the ice cream parlor treating them to whatever they want. He reveals to me that he had been married, and has three sons. Although still married the union had been broken, they have been living separately for ten years. She lives in New York with two of their sons; the eldest still resides in Jamaica. He has assured me that the marriage has been over for years, explaining several incidents which led to the breakup of the union. The different views and way of discipline administered to the children have been a major factor in their frequent arguments and disagreements, which ultimately led to the years of separation. I sympathized with him over the loss of his family, but am careful never to encourage him to make the separation final with divorce. If that is to be done it should be his decision. There is no need to look long to see that Norris is a much older man than I am. I have not asked his age, summarizing that he may be in his thirties. He has taken on the task of teaching me to dance, and the art of consuming alcohol. The lessons begin with gin and tonic. I get accustomed to the strange taste, liking it. I love the feeling of abandonment and exhilaration it gives me. Soon I graduate from gin and tonic to vodka and orange juice. I'm a good student excelling in the sadistic and addictive act of "holding my liquor." With great pride I graduate to scotch on the rocks. Scotch especially undiluted with anything except the melting ice is a little harder to swallow, but under his skillful hands I'm soon able to drink any man under the table." My capacity to tolerate the consumption of large amounts of alcohol frightens me, but those thoughts are quickly pushed to the back of my mind as I drink and dance swaying to music every weekend. The term "designated driver" has never been heard of, but someone surely needs to be designated to drive, as we leave the clubs early Saturday and Sunday mornings at times weaving down the streets throwing our heads back in uncontrollable mirth as he drives me home. But it's fun; I'm slowly becoming addicted to this newfound freedom.

    My children now see very little of me on the weekends. After coming home late on Friday and Saturday nights I try spending time with them on Sunday, but the hangover from the previous night's drinking keep me in a fog. Then almost as soon as I revive to the point of being able to meet their needs, Norris shows up again ready to

# The Odyssey of Survival

whisk me off to another playground. When I refuse citing the need to do the children's laundry or prepare meals, he quickly asks what the cost would be for my sisters to do the chores for me. My sisters in turn gladly state a price, and I'm free to go.

Jessica begins resenting this new intrusion in her life robbing her of my presence. The trips to the ice cream parlor are no longer enjoyable for her. She flatly refuses to be placated with any treats from him.

On more than one occasion my sisters have plans of their own leaving us with no adult supervision for the girls. My need to get out is so great that I take the children to Chad's mother, leaving them in her care while we head off to some event of simply to meet friends as we bar hop around town. We go as far as the west coast; Montego Bay, Negril, St. Catherine, Spanish Town and St. Ann's Bay. There's no telling where our travels will take us on any given Sunday. Wherever the party is, we find it. One Sunday afternoon we stop to get something to eat. Instead of ordering jerk chicken for me as usual, he places two orders of jerk pork. Without much cajoling I'm eating. Never before in my life have I raised a morsel of this forbidden flesh to my lips. Chewing on it, all the teachings from our parents and from church rush into my memory. I almost choke on the pork, but I ignore all the warnings. Watching me, he gloats, saying. "I got the Seventh Day Adventist to eat pork. Tell me that's not the sweetest meat you have ever eaten."

My family knows about my drinking escapades, but not one word will be uttered about the consumption of swine's flesh. I have ventured into unchartered waters, and no matter how loving and supportive my family is this cannot be told. They will not understand. We have broken all the rules of our parents and what used to be our religion, but no one has ventured out this far into the unknown. I'm ashamed to admit it.

Before our mother's departure to Canada, all the other children with the exception of the Anthon have stopped attending church. With maturity came rebellion. We rebelled against our mother's treatment of us, her betrayal of our trust to protect us from danger and abuse, her treatment of our father and of strangers. As the children matured regardless of what she threatened or did, attending church is no longer an option for us. We simply refuse to go.

Norris proudly announces to his friends his accomplishment in getting the Seventh-day Adventist to eat pork, drink alcohol and dance the nights away. I cringe inside. I'm ashamed of some of my actions, but it's too late. There is no going back now. I had become a pork eating; liquor drinking, backsliding Seventh Day Adventist. This is now a part of our weekly routine. Sometimes I request jerk chicken but Norris tells me to stop pretending to dislike his favorite meat. It is good and I know it. There is no arguing the matter. Secretly I consume jerk pork every Sunday, followed by a drink to rid my taste buds of the memory.

Three months after our first date he takes me to his home. I'm genuinely surprised at the state of the house. He lives in an upper middle class neighborhood, which doesn't surprise me. He's giving me the grand tour; the master bedroom gets my attention. It seems as if the woman of the house had recently left for work, expecting to return any minute. Her perfumes, make-up and personal items are all neatly lined up on the dresser. Her clothes are neatly hanging in the closet and a variety of shoes stand ready to be stepped into. The feeling of invading another woman's private space is overwhelming, almost as if her presence is lingering at the door watching me. I ask him why he keeps her belongings in such pristine condition if she left ten years ago. He explains that he doesn't sleep in the room, but in another bedroom, which he calls his music room, therefore he has no reason to disturb her stuff. This explanation sounds plausible and I accept it. The house tour ends and we sit down in the living room to talk. A few minutes later there is a loud knock at the gate and the three fierce German shepherd dogs in the backyard starts barking ferociously. Norris goes out the door to see what the commotion is all about. Within a few seconds I hear loud angry voices outside. I hear a woman yelling. Curiosity gets the better of me and I peek out the window. From my vantage point I see and hear her making demands to come in. She is yelling that she knows he has been courting a woman who is inside the house.

"I know that you have a woman in there. For months now you have been very evasive, I can't reach you on the telephone and you are never home. What's going on?"
"Margie I'm telling you again go home. What I do is none of your business; I'm my own big man."

"It is my business. You have been telling me you love me and I have put my life on hold for you. Now you're seeing someone else. I want to see her so I can tell her who you really are. Let me in now."

"If you come in here and the dogs bite you it's your problem. Go home and I'll talk to you tomorrow."

"I don't want to talk to you tomorrow. You are a lying, two timing bastard and I hope she finds that out before she gets hurt the way you have hurt me. This is not over. If you think you can get rid of me just like this you are wrong. I'm going to get back at you, you'll see."
With the dogs barking and her yelling, neighbors are peeking from behind their curtains. Still yelling about him being a two timer, she walks away.
Norris watches her walk away then he re-enters the house. As he is about to join me on the couch, the dogs start barking again, they run for the gate. Norris turns around, looking outside, and I go back to the window. There perched in mid stride at the top of the surrounding wall, is the woman, as she in a last ditch effort to satisfy her suspicions try to scale the wall, into the yard. The dogs lunge for her legs, which are dangling in mid air. Norris yells at the dogs to sit. Reluctantly they obey the command. Watching in horror from the confines of the house I see her trying frantically to make a speedy retreat off the wall. It's not a pretty sight. This time Norris watches until she disappears around the corner. A thousand questions race through my mind. I want answers.

## The Odyssey of Survival

He tries assuring me that there is nothing between them except for a newly formed friendship.

"Do you think I'm stupid? If there is nothing going on between both of you why would she be so angry to be willing to climb over the wall to see what's going on?"

"Honestly, there is nothing going on. We met a few weeks before I met you. We went out for drinks a couple of times. We have never been intimate and I don't know why she would come here saying all those things."

"Women do not behave like that unless you give them a reason to do so. You must have made promises to her or lied to her. Which one is it?"

"Neither. Whatever she thinks I told her is all in her head. If I wanted to be with her I would have been. Don't let her ruin the afternoon; forget about her, this won't happen again."

One month later he tells me that he has to make a trip to Miami for business. I don't know what type of business he has in Miami and refrains from asking too many questions. He discloses that he is a United States Resident, which requires him to make yearly trips to keep his status. He claims that on those trips he shops for clothes and other items. The day of his departure he picks me up from work taking me to his home. He needs help packing his bags. He's in the shower and I am folding his clothes and packing his suitcase for him. I notice his passport lying on the bed. Picking it up I read his information. He is who he says he is. I look for his birth date; it jumps off the page at me. I blink my eyes looking again. Are my eyes playing tricks on me? Are my eyes sending the correct information to my brain? Looking again I focus on the year - 1933. He was born in 1933. How old does that make him?

# The Odyssey of Survival

I do the math, but I refuse to believe the answer. When I hear the shower turn off I return the passport to its place and continue packing his bags. But my mind is consumed with this information. He could not be that old. His brother comes to take him to the airport and we secure the home leaving the dogs in the care of a family friend. On the way to the airport they drop me off at my home. Immediately I grab paper and a pencil doing the math again. No it still has to be incorrect. I ask my sisters to do the calculation and they give me the same answer. I have been going out with a man who is twice my age.

I'm twenty-four years old and he is forty-eight. He could easily be my father. I'm thrown into frenzy. What should I do when he returns in a couple weeks? What am I going to do then, should I continue seeing him?

With Norris gone I spend my weekends with my girls. They are happy to have me back to themselves. I had become so consumed with having a good time that the children had been neglected. Trekking all over the Island had blinded my eyes to their needs. They are growing up so fast we need to relish every moment with them. We take them to the zoo, the botanical gardens, to the beach and to the movies. Two weeks later Norris returns from Miami. He drops his bags off at his home and makes a beeline to mine. We are happy to see him back. He had become a regular visitor, even playing board games with us at times. I think he misses his family and receives some sort of satisfaction being with us. I decide to leave the age issue alone; At least for now. Our friendship resumes, but I curtail my absence from my home. Instead of being gone every weekend I go out twice per month. Spending more time with the children as promised. We fall into a comfortable routine. As the months pass by we're acutely aware that the time for our mother's return from Canada is fast approaching. I have not decided whether to resume living in the apartment or find a new place. What I do know is that as soon as she returns, I'm out of here.

The mailman delivers the letter containing the dreaded news. Mother will be returning home in six weeks.

"But God – so rich is he in his mercy because of and in order to satisfy the great and wonderful and intense love with which he loved us.
Even when we were dead by our shortcomings and trespasses, He made us alive together in fellowship and in union with Christ. It is by his grace that you are saved.
And he raised us up together with Him and made us sit down together in the heavenly sphere in Christ Jesus.
He did this that he might clearly demonstrate through the ages to come the immeasurable riches of his free grace, kindness and goodness of heart toward is in Christ Jesus."
Ephesians 2: 4-7

# The Odyssey of Survival

***Life question:*** *Freedom is never free, there is always a price attached to the privileges we enjoy. Someone must pay that price. This time I have made my own choices. The price has not been exacted yet – but I'm under no illusion that I'll have to pay. Do you believe Norris' story that he s has been separated for ten years? I believe him, but there is a nagging doubt deep within my soul telling me that all is not as he portrays it to be. Should I run now or wait around for proof?*

*What would you do?*

**Answer:**

## Chapter Sixteen

## MOTHER'S WRATH

Mother's return will drastically change our lives. For two years we have experienced total freedom, it's about to be yanked away. The harmony and bliss will be replaced with tension, stress, fighting, yelling and verbal abuse; all negative. There is nothing positive with her. Why does she have to come back? We are not looking forward to her return. But regardless of what we think or how we feel, the date is fast approaching and adjustments must be made.

Cheryl has formed a relationship with a young man in the neighborhood named Malik. He loves her daughter Nadine, frequently visiting to play and bring her treats. A wholesome atmosphere exists. We tell Norris and Malik about our mother's impending return from Canada. Malik, being from the neighborhood knows her, but Norris had never had the privilege of making her acquaintance. This prospect scares me. But there is no avoiding the reality of the situation. They will have to be introduced. The dreaded day draws closer. Oh God, its today. Norris graciously agrees to give me a ride to the airport to pick her up. With great trepidation we wait for the time to leave home to make the trip. It's as if a gloom of death has been cast over the household. Such a great contrast exists between her departure and her return. If we had control over the sun, this day would never dawn.

Reluctantly we leave for the airport. There is no joy in my heart. I struggle to tell Norris about her disposition without divulging family secrets. He has a difficult time understanding what I'm trying to tell him. After all, people love their mothers and miss them when they are absent. He thinks we should be ecstatic at her return. But he doesn't know and cannot understand the family dynamics.

# The Odyssey of Survival

Air Canada airline arrives on schedule. I hope against hope that she had missed the flight in Toronto, but am not that lucky. My heart sinks when as the passengers claim their luggage, I see her. Pointing her out to Norris I plaster a smile on my face as she approaches us. We greet and hug. She looks good, seems that she enjoyed her extended vacation. I wish she had made a permanent change of address, but how could I wish this awful fate upon Amelia and her household in Canada? She is introduced to Norris who receives a cold stare, she barely acknowledges his presence. Embarrassment washes over me. We load her luggage in the car and begin the drive home. An awkward silence permeates the car. Several times I try to break the ice. After a while she starts talking about the wonderful time spent in Canada. She announces her regret having to return to Jamaica. She also confides in us that she had asked her daughters to allow her to remain in Canada, but was told by Amelia that she treasures her marriage and her being there had put enough pressure on the relationship so she could not remain there any longer. Poor Amelia; I can only imagine the hell her household had experienced during the past two years. For her marriage sake, I'm happy mother left Canada. Her other daughters had flatly ignored her request.

From Amelia we learn how she had wreaked havoc in the household, even to the point of writing to the lawyer trying to sabotage the process of little Crystal becoming a Canadian citizen. Mother's jealousy that Amelia had gone to such lengths to provide a better life for a sick, motherless child drove her insane. She is angry that Amelia chose to adopt Crystal, and only gave her a vacation. Thankfully Amelia is able to deal with the legal issues and help the child. Amelia's private household business was told to neighbors and friends. While Amelia is at work mother makes it her business to go through her private documents. She checked her bank accounts, she re-arrange her personal belongings and generally made a nuisance of herself. Amelia's husband becomes very uncomfortable with his mother-in-law in their home. He changes his work schedule, leaving home quite early in the mornings, returning late at nights. His home, which had been his castle and his refuge, has become a place to be avoided.

# The Odyssey of Survival

In Canada, Patricia gives birth to a daughter, she refuses to allow mother in her home, or to make her granddaughter's acquaintance. They have not spoken since the telephone conversation they had just after Patricia left Jamaica years earlier. Patricia refused to visit Amelia's home during the two years mother stayed there. The trauma of finding out her true identity on the airplane to Canada is still painfully fresh in her mind. She has not forgiven her and can't pretend that it's okay. Mother's welcome in Canada had been short lived. One would have thought that with four daughters and twelve grandchildren living in the country, she would have been welcomed even in one place. The opposite was true. In every home she visits she tries controlling the daughter and taking over the running of the household. She wants to tell her daughters how to care for their husbands, while criticizing the husband on his control over his home. She rearranges the kitchen cupboards and linen closets, making them to her liking. She changes the bedtime of the children, the previously acceptable television programs are forbidden and meal times are changed to her preference. Every home is turned upside down. Now she is back in Jamaica. Lucky us! This is her home, so we can in no wise turn her away. If we don't like her rules, we can leave. We survived childhood, becoming self- sufficient adults. Listening to her recount her stay in Canada brings a smile to my face. From her point of view it was perfectly idyllic.

At home the rest of the gang has done a great job making the house appear welcoming for her. We had cooked a meal, and cleaned the house until it shone. Hopefully she'll find nothing to complain about. The car pulls up at the gate and her grandchildren run out to greet her, as we carry in her bags. The others paint smiles on their faces, mustering up their courage to make the approach. We succeed in making her feel welcome as she struts into her domain to resume ruling with what had been an iron hand. Politely we listen to her escapades. She tells us about the wonderful places she had visited, the vastness of the foreign land, the six lane highways where cars sped along at the unbelievable speed of sixty-five miles per hour. She elaborates about the beautiful homes of our sisters. The bone chilling cold of winter, snow piled as high as the covered cars, and the searing heat of summer. She tells of the beautiful snow capped mountains and snow laden trees of Niagara Falls in all its glory as it cascades down the rocks emptying itself into the Lake. We are genuinely happy that she had been given such a wonderful opportunity to get off the island, visit new places, and enjoy new experiences. But as usual her pleasantries are short lived. Her story telling comes to an end. And she inquires about our welfare. We assure her that we are well. She turns her attention to me, then to Norris.

"And who would this gentleman be?"

"He is a very good friend of mine."

To the total astonishment of everyone in the room, my mother looks at the man she had recently met saying to him, "Be careful of your friendship and your feelings for her, because she changes men as often as you change your socks."

Absolute humiliation; Total embarrassment; Unbelievable shame; Hate; loathe and fury seethes through my body. I shiver from head to toe and back again causing angry tears to sting my eyes. Goose pimples rise on my flesh. Adrenalin pumps through my veins and my lips tremble with anger. For the second time in my life, because of her, I wish the ground would open up and swallow me. My concern is Norris. What is he thinking? How will he react? What will be his decision regarding me after hearing this from my own mother? The air is so thick with apprehension it can be cut with a knife. Looks of shock dumfounds my sisters as they all look at me with pity in their eyes. I open my mouth to offer some unknown explanation to Norris, but sensing my discomfort and seeing my pain he takes my hand in his.

"It's okay you don't have to explain anything. I'll go now. We'll talk later."

I walk him to his car, trying to explain why she would make such a remark, making excuses for my mother. He simply assured me.

## The Odyssey of Survival

"It is all right, forget about it. What she said does not change how I feel about you."

Promising to speak with me the next day he leaves. I'm so angry with her. Nothing hidden in the bags interests me; I walk away seeking refuge in my old room. This is the clincher. My answer is clear. I definitely will not be remaining here now that she is back. There is no normalcy for life to return to. When a prisoner has been given his freedom, it is awfully foolish of him to voluntarily return to captivity. I need a new apartment. Moving day is imminent. She tries exerting her control over us again, but too much has happened during the time she had been gone. Even so some respect must be shown to her so we adjust ourselves and try falling back into stride. It's not easy. The one thing, which will absolutely not happen, is for us to attend church, Anton has continued going. The rest of us want no part of her religion or her God.

Conflicts arise daily between us. We literally rub each other the wrong way. She is critical of everything I do, from the way I indulge or discipline my children to the fact that I am going out with an older man. She disapproves of my weekend outings and complains bitterly if my sisters are not home and the children are left with her. In an effort to alleviate the pressure I curtail my outings. She develops a love/hate attraction to Norris. In his presence she drips with honey while in his absence she turns the dagger in his back. She constantly tells me he's only using me, that I am only an old man's past time. Usually I ignore her, but one day her comments are so blistering that I have to say something.

"You are just jealous because someone likes me. You hate us because you have become a has-been, and we are young, beautiful, and have the world at our feet."

"You think you're all that, it is only because of me that any of you are here, and I can still take out any one of you that I choose. Go on, keep thinking that all is well, when you think its all peace and safety it is going to be sudden destruction."

# The Odyssey of Survival

She has never been short on unpleasant surprises. She is as unpredictable and unstable as the waves of the ocean. No one knows when or where she will rise up or crash down upon our heads. Life with her has regained its hellish qualities. We must get out of her house.

It's Sunday afternoon and Norris is here to pick me up to attend a party with him. My sisters have agreed to care for my girls. Just before Norris arrives mother disappears upstairs. I have no idea what she's up to. Norris comes in, greets the girls –handing over candy and treats. We hear mother's voice at the top of the stairs. All eyes turn upwards. To our great astonishment, there at the top of the stairs, poised in the flirtatious stance of a stripper stands our mother wearing the shortest shorts and midriff blouse of a teenager.

"Norris," she utters in a coy tone, "Why would you want her, when you can have me? She has no idea how to please a man like you. I can take you to places you have never been to, and make you feel the way you deserve to feel."

Is there no end to this woman? With mouths gaping we look up at her in disbelief. Her fifty- seven years old body, that has borne fifteen children, sashays down the stairs. Fluttering her eyes at him, she sensuously rubs her hands over her sagging, stretched mark filled, distended stomach. We look at her fried eggs flat breast, barely concealed by the skimpy shirt, her lumpy cellulite packed legs, and huge hips pushes against the too tight shorts she has no business wearing. The sight of her is disgusting.

"Mama what are you doing? Go back upstairs and put some clothes on." She ignores me presenting herself in front of Norris. She repeats her question.

"She is just a girl why would you want her instead of me? She has no idea how to please a man."

# The Odyssey of Survival

I want to kill her as hateful thoughts and ways to get rid of her race through my mind. "Norris let's go." I manage to mutter. Throwing her a look filled with venom, we walk out the door. She watches from the doorway as he opens the passenger door for me to get in, and then slams her door. I'm in tears as soon as the door closes. What can I say to him? How do I explain away the behavior of my mother? Should I tell him that she has a mental problem? Maybe that will explain her erratic behavior. Or should I just tell him how she has been trying to kill us since birth. What would he do if I told him how she had sold me to Uncle Duke for years? Would he understand any of it? Would he still want to be with me if he knew the truth about my life? She had not succeeded in killing us, and has now embarked upon a crusade to ruin our lives. None of my thoughts are expressed.

"Your mother is just a little jealous that you girls are having a good time. She probably had a hard life when she was at this age. Don't worry about it and don't take it so seriously, she is just having some fun."

If he only knew how much I needed to worry about it. This is no fun, all out war has just been declared between us. If she was going to begin making passes at Norris then mother and daughter has entered a new phase in our relationship. She has her husband. Daddy is very much alive and well. I guess the prospect of a younger man entices her. Well she is not going to win this war. I decide then and there to remain in her home, flaunt my relationship in her face and watch her make a fool of herself. Two can play the game.

Making myself more available to Norris increases my absence from home. Now the partying begins on Friday nights. We meet friends at designated places to eat roast fish, drink beer and alcohol and jam to reggae music. I sleep most of Saturday; get up to care for the girls, leaving later to dance and drink the night away at a nightclub. Sunday afternoons are spent visiting friends and drinking more alcohol. This is now my weekly routine. Mother's objections to my life style fall on deaf ears. What she says or does means absolutely nothing to me. I'm out of control. Defiance is my main objective.

# The Odyssey of Survival

Rebellion against everything she pretends to stand for runs hot in my veins. One Friday night after the usual reveling, Norris takes me home. My key turns in the lock but the door remains locked; pushing at it I realize that another lock has been added. I knock. One of my sisters comes to unlock the door. Mother threatens her with death if she dares to open it. Norris sits in his car watching and waiting to see me safely enter the house. Realizing I have a problem he gets out of his car to help. From her upstairs bedroom window she yells.

"Get away from my door you little slut, I don't want you in my house. Go back where you are coming from." Looking up at her in the window I reply.

"That's no problem, I'll gladly go back." I walk out the gate and back into the car. Norris takes me home with him. This begins a new phase of our relationship.

When I return home Saturday afternoon she calls me every name in the book. I wonder aloud what pastor had preached at church earlier. She scorns me for what she assumes had taken place in Norris's bed. She provided that opportunity by locking me out of the house. I'm certainly not about to sleep under the stars. I had a very enjoyable night and nothing she says will erase the smile from my face. If she locks me out again I know where another bed waits to welcome me, as a matter of fact I will personally take every opportunity to return to his bed. Eventually she learns to ignore me even feigning blindness to my existence. For my children's sake I make adjustments to my lifestyle, paying more attention to their needs than to my mother's disapproval of me. I don't know how, but she finds out where Norris operates his business, his address and his martial status. Daily mother taunts me about my involvement with a married man. I try explaining the years of separation to her, but she won't listen.

"He is not divorced and therefore he is still a married man. It wasn't so long ago that another married man's wife tried to kill you. This time I will personally deliver you to his wife to beat the skin off your black ass."

"They are not together, she lives in America and they have been separated for ten years."

"Believe that if you want to. Tell him to make an honorable woman out of you and marry you. You already have two children for two different men, is this the way you plan to live the rest of your life?"

Norris makes another visit to Miami. She overhears me telling my sisters where he went and jumps right in.

"See what I told you, he's gone to visit his wife in America leaving you here to feed his dogs." I'm not feeding his dogs but her words make me wonder whether or not he has been telling me the truth about his situation. I vow to find out as soon as he returns.

He returns and I ask no questions, if anything we become inseparable. The girls love him; Even Jessica has warmed up to him, and my sisters think he's wonderful. His age is a non-issue except to my mother. Constantly she refers to it, and I lend a deaf ear. She has a problem with every man we speak with. She not only hates us but also resents anyone who shows interest in any of us. It will be her greatest joy if all eleven children remain unattached, unsuccessful, unmarried, uneducated, dependent individuals, remaining in the trenches groveling with her like dogs for the scraps falling from the table, so she can kick us around, spitting in our faces. Our efforts to succeed or form relationships only serve to anger her. She finds every way imaginable and unimaginable to embarrass us and destroy our friendships, especially if the relationship is with a member of the opposite sex.

# The Odyssey of Survival

Cheryl has become friendly with Malik. Their friendship progresses to the next level. They are in love with each other. He adores her daughter, Nadine, and she calls him daddy. They are talking about getting married. Our parents know about their relationship and for the most part consent to it. Malik does the right thing; he comes to the house with a plan in mind. Sitting down with them, he professes his love for Cheryl, asking for her hand in marriage. They give their approval and blessing. Excitement fills the house. We have a wedding to plan. The engagement party is scheduled for a Saturday evening two weeks later at Malik's home. I tell Norris about the party, but didn't invite him.

Everything is in place for a good time. Our little sister is going to get married and she has the support of the family. Or so we think.

The party will begin at 5pm. Malik arrives at 4:30 pm to pick up Cheryl. He has no idea the trauma that Cheryl and the rest of the household have been experiencing for the last couple hours. At about 3:00 pm mother announces that over her dead body, Cheryl would leave the house to go any place, especially not to attend her own engagement party. We look from one to the other trying to figure out what had happened to bring about this strange reaction. We try our hardest to get an answer from her about why the sudden turn in her mood, but she offers no explanation for her irrational decision. To make matters worse she announces that none of us will be allowed to leave the house. Not one of us was going to be allowed out the door. At first we laugh commenting on how crazy she is. Soon we realize that this is no laughing matter. Frantically we try reasoning with her to even allow Cheryl to go. Guests are waiting to share in her joy. Lots of money has been spent for the occasion, but she adamantly refuses to listen to reason. No one knows exactly what happened to trigger this behavior. We know we are threading on very dangerous grounds. She has not only forbidden any of us to leave the house, but with a sharpened machete across her knees, she places herself in a chair by the door. Locking the door, she removes the key from the lock. With a glazed look in her eyes she dares any one of us to attempt taking the key from her. Losing a limb or a life would be a sure thing. We plea,

## The Odyssey of Survival

beg and yell. Cheryl cries. The children get upset and they start crying. The dog is barking and we are yelling. She ignores all of us. The engagement party will go on without the fiancée. This evening, without a shadow of a doubt, we come to the realization that what we have joked about all our lives is a reality. Our mother is crazy.

Malik is coming through the gate, she shouts at him through the window. "Malik do not come any further, if you take one more step into my yard I will kill you." In astonishment and confusion he stops in his tracks.

"What's going on? I'm here to get Cheryl for the party."

"Why you are here is of no concern to me, get off my property before I have you arrested for trespassing."

He presses on telling her that the party needs to get started, almost all the guests have arrived, and everyone is waiting for Cheryl to get there.

"For the last time I am telling you to get off my property. There will be no engagement party tonight or any other night for as long as I live. Cheryl is going nowhere with you, if she leaves this house tonight I will kill her and you. Now get out of my yard and don't come back."

Malik is bewildered. What has gone wrong? Cheryl approaches the window. Mother comes up behind her shoving her away, pulling and closing the curtain. By now the neighbors hearing raised voices; begin gathering on the street to see what is going on. Malik starts talking with the next-door neighbor about our mother's behavior. The neighbor offers to try talking to her and comes through the gate. "Miss Mac what's going on? Why are you refusing to let the young people get engaged? Come out here so we can talk." Flinging the window open she yells. "You people are going to let me commit murder tonight. Miss Lee, go home and stay out of my business, and you boy, go home to your mother." Inside the house we group together devising a plan to surprise her from behind yanking the machete away from her

# The Odyssey of Survival

then grabbing the key. One at a time we get close to her, taking up our positions on opposite sides. She senses our intention and raises the machete above her head wildly spinning around chopping at any and everything within reach. None of us want to be killed by an insane person so we abort the plan. Helplessly we watch as she single handedly ruin what should have been one of the happiest days in Cheryl's life.

Malik finally gives up and drives away. Fresh sobbing comes from Cheryl as she watches him leave knowing her future had just died an untimely death. Malik has the unpleasant task of explaining to his family and friends what has happened and why the engagement party was not going to happen. Hours later when she is sure that it was too late for the party to happen, she relinquishes her post at the door, throws the keys on the floor telling us to do whatever the hell we want to do. Quickly we grab the keys, open the door and fly out of the house, trying to understand what had happened. Curious neighbors stand around wandering what will happen next. Taking Nadine with her Cheryl runs to Malik's home seeking what she hopes to be refuge from this craziness. From her upstairs bedroom window mother sees Cheryl going down the street. She runs down the stairs and out the door yelling her name. Cheryl turns around and mother shouts. "I don't care where you go but leave that child right here." Cheryl, at this point, wants nothing to do with her, much less leave her child who is already upset.

Turning on her heels, Cheryl continues walking away. Mother rushes up behind her and tries grabbing Nadine's hand, as she tries to pull her out of her mother's arms. Cheryl whirls around, holding her child closer to her chest. A fight begins between mother and daughter for Nadine who is bawling at the top of her voice. Mother pulls at her flaring legs and Cheryl hangs on to her for dear life. We run to our sister. In the middle of the street with all the neighbors looking on we wrestle with our mother to loosen her grip on Nadine. She holds on with the grip of a lioness and Cheryl hugs her crying baby to her chest crushing the very air out of her lungs. Everyone is screaming at the top of his voice, creating one of the most disgraceful scenes I have ever witnessed. What a disgrace! We will never be able to hold up our heads in the neighborhood again. A street fight with our mother. What have befallen this family?

No one wants to reenter the house; it no longer feels like home, more like a dungeon in which evil dwells. I take my children by their hands and we walk as far away as we could. My girls, between sobs ask for Nadine. "She's with her mom." I tell them. "You'll see her later." As dusk turns to dark I know I have to retrace my steps and take the children home. Walking back I'm deep in thought. I know that our time in this place is over. I can no longer continue living with my children under these volatile and unstable circumstances. Mother has locked herself in her bedroom chanting and praying at the top of her voice, for the death and destruction of all of us.

At sunrise the following morning she walks into the backyard pulls out her breast and begins beating on them. She holds a lit match to the nipples; while imploring God to rid her of her afflictions. The situation is hopeless. Watching her, we come to the conclusion that it's too risky to leave the children with her during the day so I decide to take time off from work to find a new place to live. With a tear stained face, Cheryl returns taking Nadine to bed with her. There is no telling what a crazed mind will do next. That her reasoning makes sense to no one but herself is irrelevant.

Cheryl is miserable. No amount of support and compassion has been able to ebb the flow of tears. She has been humiliated by her mother in front of the person she loves and now to make it worse his family, after hearing what had happened to prevent the engagement, is adamant that Malik stop seeing her. They are furious about the wasted money, embarrassed about having to explain the situation to their family and friends, and have given Malik an ultimatum to stop seeing the daughter of a crazy woman or else… We are all deeply embarrassed. We don't want to be in the house, and are too ashamed to venture outside of it. The whispers of the neighbors can be heard when we walk down the streets. We hang our heads low with shame. Like the troopers we have learned to become, we continue with our

# The Odyssey of Survival

lives, not knowing what will happen next. The week drags on. Tempers flare easily, and the atmosphere is thick with impending doom. We know something else, just as awful is going to happen, but have no idea of what, when, or on whom the hatchet will fall. If we could have been given one small peek into the future we would have been better prepared for the next tragedy.

"In him we also were made God's heritage and we obtained an inheritance; for we had been foreordained in accordance with His purpose, which works out everything in agreement with the counsel and design of His will.
So that we who first hoped in Christ live for the praise of his glory.
In him you also who have heard the Word of Truth, the glad tidings of your salvation, and have believed in and adhered to and relied on Him, were stamped with the seal of the long promised Holy Spirit.
That spirit is the guarantee of our inheritance, in anticipation of its full redemption and our acquiring possession of it – to the praise of His glory."
Ephesians 1: 11-14
(AKJV)

# The Odyssey of Survival

***Life question:*** *The command to honor your father and mother that your days would be long upon the land was very hard to keep. How could it be possible for children to honor a mother who displayed such unsavory behavior? This had not been brought on as punishment for some misconduct of the child. It was a blatantly planned activity to ruin a young lady's life. Does God still expect honor to be shown to a mother who behaves like this? Should we try harder to understand her? But how can you relate to someone who is bent on your destruction? What are we supposed to do? What would Jesus do?*

***Answer:***

## Chapter Seventeen

## HOMELESS

Still reeling from the events of the previous week, we speak in hushed voices about the total embarrassment. We are still trying to comfort Cheryl, but to no avail. Malik has been forbidden by his family to see her and she is devastated. The children have been traumatized. Nadine huddles close to her mother, afraid to leave her side.

Norris comes by and I jump into his car, begging him to drive away as fast and go as far as possible from 26 Defoe Avenue. Even then, I am careful to avoid mentioning what transpired over the weekend, fearful that he will sever the relationship with the daughter of a crazed woman. If he makes that choice no one will blame him. After all, why would anyone choose to associate themselves with the likes of us? I begin asking co-workers if they know of an apartment for rent. My brother has settled into my former apartment and I don't think it's fair to disrupt his life asking him to give it back to me, besides; I want to get out of the neighborhood. This is no longer a place to be. My children need to be in a better environment away from the stigma of being related to Mrs. Macaroon. We don't just have any mother to contend with. We have a hateful, vile, jealous, demon possessed, crazy person. We survived our childhood. Now we have to survive her into adulthood. To do so is easier than before; all we have to do is get out of her house. We're weary of the tension in the household. Curiously we wait to see if she will get dressed and go to church on Sabbath pretending to be pious, good and holy. Sure enough she does. Dressed in white to sing in the choir, she clamps her hat on her head, secures her Bible under her arms, pick up her purse, stuffs her feet into her white pumps, and without speaking a word to any of us, waltzes out the front door to church.

If God were like man, he would smite her dead. But He doesn't and we know that our freedom will last only for a few hours. She'll return soon.

I again tell Norris not to pick me up over the weekend. I'm not in the mood to go drinking and dancing, we have serious decisions to make. In her absence we talk freely, planning to find a house rent it and all of us who work share the expenses. Anton will remain at home. This sounds like a good idea. Tomorrow we'll buy a newspaper and search the classifieds. With a plan in place some of our gloom disappears and a pinpoint of light appears at the far end of a very long and dark tunnel.

Completing our chores on Sunday, we prepare to walk out to the corner shop to buy a newspaper. We hear voices in the living room and go to see who is here. It's Lester, our older brother. In her words mother tells him how we tried beating her out of the house a few days ago. She turns everything around making herself the victim of our terror. She tells her son that she had to grab a machete to protect herself from us because we wanted to capture her house so that we and our father could live in it after putting her out.

"That's not true." I interrupt. "We were trying to go to Cheryl's engagement party and she locked us all in, including Cheryl so that none of us could go. She kept threatening to kill anyone of us who came close enough to the door. Malik came to get Cheryl and she wouldn't let her go, she even threatened to kill him if he came through the gate, now Malik has stopped talking to Cheryl because his family told him that if he continues talking to her they'll have nothing to do with him."

"Mama came to me crying that she is fearful for her life and afraid to sleep at night because you, Marcia has threatened to kill her in her sleep. She asked me to come here today to remove all of you from her house so she can sleep at night and be at peace."

"Lester Mama is lying. She's the one who keeps telling us that she's going to pour hot oil in our ears while we're asleep. She's the one who went crazy last week Saturday night bringing down disgrace on the family when she ran down the street after Cheryl grabbing Nadine from her while screaming at the top of her lungs."

"I don't care what happened. The only thing I know is that mama came to me crying that she is afraid to live in her own home with all of you here so I'm here to put you all out of her house."

"What do you mean you are here to put us out of the house? This is where we live. We have no place to go."

"That is going to be your problem. All of you need to leave now."
"Are you crazy? Leave to where?"

"All of you get out of here now. Mama wants all of you out, and I'm here to help her do it. Get out of here. Get your junk and your pickneys and get out of here. This poor woman has worked all her life and now she can't sleep in peace in her own house. None of you is going to spend one more night in here."

"This is our father's house. You can't throw us out. We have a right to be here if we want to. She has already thrown out Daddy; he was here like a squatter in his own home. And now she wants to throw us out. And who are you? Where did you come from ordering us out of here? You don't know anything about what happened. We did nothing to her. This is not fair."

"I'm not here to argue with any of you. If you don't get out of here I will personally throw each one of you out." Screaming at us to get out of his mother's house Lester moves towards us. Mother begins laughing, egging him on.

"Throw all of them out. Get them out of my house. I don't want them here let them go find their pa and live with him. I hate all of them; get them all out of my sight. See I have help.

# The Odyssey of Survival

You all thought you could beat me out of here but who's laughing now. Ha ha! Get out of my house you bastards."

Lester moves through the house grabbing our stuff throwing it outside. Mother runs upstairs empties our drawers, yanks our clothing from the closets throwing armfuls of clothing outside. We're screaming, the children are crying, mother is singing and Lester is telling us to hurry up and get out. Within one hour of Lester's arrival all the earthly possessions of eight people are strewn all over the front yard and into the street. Between both of them they push us out the door and through the gate into the street. Eight of us stand there with no idea what to do. Mother picks up the clothing in the yard throwing them at our feet, locking the gate with a padlock. She then goes back into the house slamming and locking the door. Should we have fought back? Should we have hit our mother pushing her out of the way? Maybe we should have grabbed our stuff from her or pushed her down the stairs? We can't fight Lester; he's much bigger and stronger than all of us put together. We didn't hit, push or curse our mother, we tried defending ourselves to our brother but he didn't believe us. Instead he believed mother's lies. Now we are standing on the streets with three children to provide shelter for. What are we going to do? The neighbors are all out looking, talking and laughing at us. We ask each other the question on every mind. "What are we going to do? We have no definite answers.

The five Macaroon children have become homeless; we have no extended family. Mother has carefully disassociated us from all family members in another attempt to ensure secrecy. When we tried making contact with one of her sisters who lives nearby, she told us. "I want nothing to do with Vira's children. I have nothing against you guys but if we build a relationship your mother will find out and I do not want her in my life." We have no grandparents. The venerable Miss Ruby has no interest in us. We don't know where to find our father.

Years ago Miss Ruby had showed up at the house in a state of anger. That was the first and only time we met our grandmother. An argument ensued between them, and much to our surprise, this petite woman of advanced years jumped up on a chair, and swiftly and resolutely slapped the face of her 50+-year-old daughter in the presence of her husband and children. The sound of the contact with flesh echoed through the room, followed by her warning.

"Gal, who do you think you are talking to? Do you think you are too old for me to whip your ass? Don't let me have to return here to fix your business. You can be as old as a horse, until the day you die; you will always be a child to me."

This was the first time of our lives that we witnessed our mother being humiliated. With mouths wide open we stared at the scene between mother and daughter, as it unfolded before our eyes. We made no comment, just watched in awe. What are we going to do? There is no one to call, no place to go. The children are crying. We are all crying. The neighbors are sympathetic, but no one dares to offer help. She will probably burn his or her house to the ground if anyone takes in or offer assistance to even the smallest child.

# The Odyssey of Survival

"Finally my brethren be strong in the Lord, and in the power of his might.
Put on the whole armor of God that you may be able to stand against the wiles of the devil.
For we wrestle not against flesh and blood, but against principalities, against powers, against the rulers of the darkness of this world, against spiritual wickedness in high places.
Therefore take upon you the whole armor of God that you may be able to withstand in the evil day, and having done all to stand."
Ephesians 6: 10-13 (KJV)

***Life question****: Another thing we had always been told was that, "I can kill any one of you and get away with it, because I have quick-silver in my head." We have no idea what this means. Was she really crazy? And O God, have any of us inherited her mental disorder? Is this our heritage? Can God bring about a miracle? Can any good come out of this family?*

**Answer:**

## Chapter Eighteen

## FINDING REFUGE

What a calamity. Woefully we survey our belongings, and the enormity of the crisis which has befallen us becomes clear. We have to find shelter, the children have to be cared for, and night is quickly approaching. We begin tossing ideas around to each other. Who can we call, where can we go? Located at the end of the block is a payphone, We search through our purses for address books and phone numbers of people whom we may be able to spend a few days with until we sort ourselves out.

Leaving everything where they are on the street, the band of eight walk to the payphone. Bridget calls a friend who shows up shortly to get her. Janice walks a few blocks to friends in the neighborhood asking for their assistance. They agreed to let her stay with them and show up with paper and plastic bags helping to stuff her belongings into them. Cheryl, swallowing her pride, walks to Malik's parent's home. She tells them what has happened to us and asked for accommodations. They grudgingly tell her they could let her sleep on the couch, but her child was not welcome, they had no room for a child and neither were they prepared to have a small child crying in their home. I tell her to go ahead I'll take care of Nadine. Anton has no one to call, no place to go. Much to my chagrin I have no choice but to call my godfather. I tell him what had happened and ask if I could stay there with the three children. He struggles with the decision, but eventually agrees telling me that the living arrangement could not last long. I promise to get out as soon as possible. He tells me to take a taxi and come up. Anton has no place to go so I take him along with me. Before separating we kiss each other holding on long and hard not wanting to sever our bond. Our lives are tethering on the brink of disaster. We have no idea what is going to happen to any of us. On this fateful Sunday evening in 1981, our family is irrevocably broken apart.

# The Odyssey of Survival

We struggle to let go of one another. When we could, we went our separate ways, crying our hearts out for our uncertain future, for our separation, and, for our shattered lives. We became separated from one another's presence, but never from our hearts.

That Sunday afternoon was the last day that any of us lived in that house. It was the last morning we woke up in that house, the last day any one of us put a glass of water to our lips in that house. None of us have trodden the stairs leading to the bedrooms. The place, which had housed us for fourteen years, in the space of one hour, became a forbidden dungeon. Never again will we sit down to a meal at the dining table. Before becoming separated, we decided that we will never return to that place. We would never speak to her again. Mother has gotten her wish and succeeded in getting us out of her house. Now we'll leave her to enjoy her own misery. The taxi stops at the gate. I get out opening the gate so the driver could drive up to the back door. With a strained smile Uncle Duke greets us; Anton is helping me unload the taxi. He asks if the cab will be taking my brother back down the hill, I lied, telling him yes, he had only accompanied me to help with the children. We'll have to devise a plan to keep him here. Living in his home is just as bad as where we came from. But we have no choice. The children have been settled down and I sit down to talk with him. He wants to know what happened at home to cause the breakdown, I try reliving the episode, but it's too fresh and way too painful to relive. I gloss over the details. Tentatively, I ask if Anton could be allowed to spend the night. Uncle Duke refuses to harbor another stray. My brain gets into gear. If Anton leaves he has no place to go, there is no way I'm going to allow my teenage brother to wander the streets. It's getting dark, I know he expects Anton to leave; excusing myself I go get him to say his goodbyes. Very quietly I give him instructions.

"Come and say goodbye to Uncle Duke, walk down the driveway, go out the gate and pretend to lock it behind you. Walk around the other side of the house, re-entering from the unlocked back door. If the dogs start barking just slip into the chauffeur's room, wait there until I come to get you."

# The Odyssey of Survival

For weeks he lives like a fugitive hiding from the authorities, sleeping in the gardeners or maids quarters. We pass food to him through the Iron Gate or if it's safe he eats his meals at the kitchen table.

The helpers have been entrusted to keep our secret. He is miserable, but at least there is a roof over his head and food in his stomach.

It's difficult getting the girls to settle down in their new surroundings. It's hard keeping them quiet, trying not to upset the peace and tranquility of the household. I am frazzled, my patience is wearing thin, but I take deep breaths, brush away the tears from my eyes and keep going. Monday morning the chauffeur is given a new job, that of transporting the children to and from school. I do as much for them as possible, not wanting to impose upon the time of the help to care for the girls. For the most part they are happy. They learn to play quietly especially when Uncle Duke or guests are in the home. I watch over them like a hawk, making it my mission to be present at all times when he talks with them. They are never left home alone in his care and Jessica, who is seven, is instructed to tell me if he ever touches her anywhere except on her hands. They are told never to sit on his lap and never ever to enter his bedroom. Maybe I'm paranoid, but I didn't care. I know firsthand what he is capable of. I promise myself to use one of his own guns which he has taught me to fire, to kill him if he ever touches any of these innocent girls. He keeps his filthy hands off them and we make the most of the situation, being grateful for a place to lay our heads at night. After a while Anton begins staying with friends from church and stops coming by daily. I miss him terribly. He is my only link with my family. But I'm happy that he has found a place to call home, even for a short time.

We communicate with one another as often as possible. No one is sleeping on the streets, and although no situation is ideal we are all working with what is available. Cheryl misses her daughter and visits on most weekends, always with Nadine screaming for her mother, becoming hysterical when she leaves. Malik did not abandon Cheryl, about six months later against the wishes of his parents; they rent an apartment and begin living together. Nadine goes to live with them.

# The Odyssey of Survival

Anton visits Daddy at his place of employment, telling him what had happened. He sends word to us that he is well. He has been staying with old friends, and he misses us terribly but is trying to endure the hardships. A few months later he sends us news that his eyes are bothering him, his blood pressure has escalated and he has been diagnosed with diabetes. My father is ill and I don't even know where he lives. With every thought of him suffering or being in need with none of his children around to hand him a glass of water. With every tear I cry on my pillow at night, and every thought of the safety and living conditions of my sisters and brother, resentment rises up in me. With every memory of how she has torn our lives apart, I hate her more. I hate the memory of her; hate the fact that she had given birth to me. I hate her very existence. My hate grows so strong that if I hear that she died I'll probably attend her funeral with one intent; *to spit on her grave.* She has finally gotten her desire; she managed to chase all of us out of the house. Now she's living large, doing as she pleases, enjoying the comforts of her paradise by herself. No one speaks to her. Daddy and his five children are out of the house, which he had worked hard to purchase and pay for. How unfair life can be. Here is a woman who has never worked one day in her entire life, had given birth to fifteen children, and left one dead husband to the mercy of hospital administration. She had traded herself for one pound of beef producing another child, had wangled herself with another innocent victim, luring him into her trap in quite the same way a spider lures a fly into its web, sucks it dry then discards the remains.

Loathing is a mild description of what I feel for her. The mention of her name causes revulsion to rise up in my stomach. I promise myself never to have anything to do with her ever again. If she needed help and depended upon me to provide it, she would die before I would stretch my hands out to her. If she depended on me to make it possible for her to see my children again she would go to her grave without them passing before her eyes. I resolved in my heart that if I saw her coming down one side of the street I'd cross to the other side, not wanting even her shadow to come in contact with mine.

# The Odyssey of Survival

If I die first and she attended my funeral I'd rise up out of the grave and slap her face. The remainder of my days will be spent without her. As far as I'm concerned she is already dead. I'm motherless.

Norris visits me often. Three months later he tells me that he has decided to permanently migrate to the United States. He had already made arrangements for the sale of his businesses and land he owns in St. Catherine. His eldest son will occupy his home. He promises that his leaving will not be the end of our relationship; he was only going ahead to make plans for us to join him soon in America. The night prior to his departure he visits to say goodbye. I will miss him. Since taking up residence on the hill we had not been able to spend any time together. I had no baby sitters so all social activities had been curtailed. He promises that his migration to the US is the first step in getting us out of Jamaica. He promises to get an apartment, find employment and make preparation for us to become a family. He tells me to get the children's passports, so we will be ready to join him there. He promised to call with a telephone number so we can keep in touch. I believe him placing all my trust in him to help us out of our predicament. He keeps his word calling me the following day giving me his telephone number. We talk frequently, making plans to be reunited. He tells me he has rented a room in the home of a woman named Bessie. He says he has told her about me, even asked her to take messages from me if I called when he was absent. She promised to do so.

Wondering why no calls had come from him for an entire week I decide to place a call to him on the weekend. Sunday afternoon, I dialed the number, Bessie answers the telephone. When I identified myself, her friendly tone changed to one of cold controlled fury.

"Hello Bessie. How are you?"

"I am fine. What do you want?"

"May I speak to Norris?"

"Norris is not home."

"Can you tell him I called, and ask him to give me a call back?"

"I will tell him no such thing and I do not want you calling my home anymore."

I'm not sure of what I heard.
"Excuse me, what did you say?" Loudly she repeats her statement.

"Norris is not home and I do not want you calling my house anymore, your calls are no longer welcome."

"Woman, do you know who I am?"

"I know who you used to be. You have been replaced, he is no longer interested in you, and his interest has shifted to me, so stop calling my house."

"Go to hell you bitch."

"No sweetheart you go to hell. Norris is now mine, so stop calling him."

I slam the telephone down, and that was the last time my fingers dialed the numbers. I wait by the phone for him to call to apologize for what she had said, even if he was lying. I need him to tell me something, but no calls come. I guess she had been right after all. I have become a used to be. I throw myself into caring for my little girls and fill the void left by Norris. My mind constantly swirls around him and the lost relationship. He was my only hope, my lifeline, and my ticket to freedom. "What's a girl to do?" The man has made his choice. Within a few months our lives become bearable to a point. We continue living with my godfather but I'm desperately trying to get out of his house. He no longer bothers me at night; he has a live-in lover and many other women and young girls satisfying his sexual appetite. But I need to establish my own household with the girls. They need stability and I need peace of mind. There is no one in Jamaica for us to turn to. I have four older sisters living in Canada. Can they help me? We have not communicated with them; therefore I have no idea how to reach them. God must have heard my prayers because even as I contemplate ways to get out of Uncle Duke's house, a better plan to get me off the Island comes about.

One day I'm called to the telephone. It's one of my sisters from Canada on the line. She asks what's been going on with the family. I tell her what had happened. Of course mother had given her a different version of the entire incident telling how we tried beating her out of her house so we could capture it. They know mother's tendencies to lie and distort the truth. Before the call ends my sister asks the most important question I have ever been asked.

"Would you like to come to Canada?"

Would I like to come to Canada? "Yes, yes, I want to come to Canada. Will you please help me?" She promises to talk to the others and get back to me soon.

Soon cannot come fast enough. Every time the telephone rings I jump to it. Is this the call? I'm walking on clouds, just the thought of getting away. Plans form in my mind of how it's going to be for the girls and myself. I'm building castles in the air, anything, anywhere, anyplace, will be better than where we are now. I pray for help to save my children.

Two weeks later the long awaited call comes. My heart skips a beat as I listen to the plans, which have been made for me to get to Canada. An invitation letter will be sent to me and immigration regulations are explained. I am ready to do whatever is necessary. Then the bad news comes. My children will have to be left behind; it's impossible for me to take them with me. Canadian Residence has to be established first. The memory of three of my sisters leaving

# The Odyssey of Survival

Jamaica comes flooding back. Each one had to leave their children behind then filing documents to get them to Canada a few years later. Can I leave my children behind? With whom will I leave them? If my children have to be left with my Mother my feet will never leave the shores of Jamaica. We will all remain right here together and continue suffering. They are never going to be placed in her care, not over my dead body. The process begins, in a couple weeks the promised documents arrive. I have to make adequate plans for my children. I tell my godfather about my sister's invitation and that I have accepted the proposal. Tearfully I sit my two daughters down to tell them what was going on. The thought of leaving them is so overwhelming that I almost abandon the idea. But it's the only way out. We have to sacrifice something to achieve what I've been hoping for; A better life for us. My very being is torn apart as I struggle to make plans to leave my children behind. They cry constantly afraid of what they know is coming. I talk with them often about the trip, its heart wrenching. If I could leave them with my sisters the departure will be easier on all of us, but thanks to a crazy woman no one is in a position to keep the girls for me. My sisters and I meet in the mall to discuss the problem. I desperately want to go, but what will become of my children? We put our heads together mapping out a workable plan. One of the suggestions is that I approach Jessica's father and his wife, asking them to care for her. We will ask Chad's mother to care for Nia. Both families are presented with my situation and asked for help with the children until I'm able to get them to Canada. Jessica's father and wife readily agreed to care for her. They have no children and will love to have her join their family. Nia's fate proves to be a little more daunting, her grandmother, works full time. Chad still lives at home but doesn't want to commit to taking responsibility for her. She is four years old and needs a mother's care. My heart is breaking, but I've fixed my eyes on the end result, getting us out of the country. This is terrible; I realize that it's only going to get harder before it gets better. I keep pressing on; I have to find someone safe with whom to leave Nia.

    A friendship had formed between Miss Baker, Nia's school's principal and myself. One morning during a conversation I mention my opportunity and desire to leave Jamaica for Canada, telling her about the dilemma of having no one with whom to leave Nia. She offers to care for my baby for me. I'm surprised at her response, questioning the reason behind her offer. She explains that she now has two children in her care whose mothers have migrated to America. She assures me that she has the space and will be more than willing to care for Nia, whom she loves. This ray of hope is discussed at length with my sisters and with Nia. Although she is only four years old we give her a voice in where and with whom she will live. Naturally she prefers to be with her mom, but she is able to grasp the meaning of what we have been explaining to her. A week later my girls and I make a trip to visit and explore the home in which Nia may be placed. Everything seems okay. She'll share a room with a five-year-old girl whose mother is in the United States. There will be no problems getting her to school; this is the principal's home.

This is far from an ideal situation. My sisters and I continue talking, contemplating our options. Regardless of how nice this woman appears to be, she is still a stranger. Can I trust her with the life of my precious little girl? My sisters and I make three more trips to Miss Baker, taking the girls with us, trying to make certain that Nia will be all right there. Finally after extensive talking, asking questions, surveying the visitors to the home, watching the interaction between Nia, and the other children, we make the decision. Nia will be left in the care of Miss Baker.

My airline ticket arrives in the mail. My departure is two weeks away. My stomach falls to my feet. While I want to go, reality is staring me in the face and I have to step up to the plate. I think of abandoning the entire idea, telling my children and sisters that I have chosen to remain with my children. But remaining in Jamaica will only mean having more children for another loser, getting into relationships for the wrong reasons and wasting my life away. No, as hard as this is going to be, I have to go through with the plans in place for my children's sake. I brought them into the world and I'll do anything to provide for them. We're all going to suffer but leaving Jamaica is the first step in the long journey to provide a better life for them. I will go through with it.

## The Odyssey of Survival

    I visit my daddy to tell him of my plans. It breaks my heart to see him in a state I have never seen him in before. His sight has deteriorated quite rapidly to the point where he needs assistance moving around the house. He recognizes us but says we appear as blurs in his vision. He is overwhelmed with joy to have his grandchildren around him. We talk about our lives, without mother and all the hardships we have endured. Before leaving his side I promise to bring him off the island if not permanently then for a vacation. Hours later we say goodbye, crying on each other's shoulders. Before leaving, I tell my daddy how much I love him, assuring him that I will never forget him.

I cry all the way home, aching for my daddy's situation and hating Mother for putting him in it. Little did I know that that was the last time I would lay eyes on my beloved father alive or dead. I have never seen my dad again. The hole in my heart is so deep that nothing have or will ever be able to fill it up, that special place reserved for him can never be filled with all the love in the world. I still miss him and will never forget the only person who has ever unconditionally, unreservedly loved me.

# The Odyssey of Survival

"But he was wounded for our transgressions, He was bruised for our guilt and iniquities; the chastisement of peace and well-being for us was upon Him, and with the stripes (that wounded) Him we are healed and made whole.
All we like sheep have gone astray, we have turned everyone to his own way; and the Lord has made to light upon Him the guilt and iniquity of us all.
He was oppressed, He was afflicted, He was submissive and opened not His mouth; like a lamb that is led to the slaughter, and as a sheep before her sharers is dumb, so He opened not His mouth."
Isaiah 53: 5-7

***Life question:*** *Is it possible for one person to have caused the disruption of so many lives? Has another person ever hated his mother the way I did? Have I committed the unpardonable sin? Could even God restore love, faith and hope in me? The wounds inflicted by my mother run so deep within our lives that we have been permanently scarred. Can I be saved? Is there hope for me? Could God save a person who hates her own mother? He had told us to love our enemies, and honor our parents. Is there hope for me?*

**Answer:**

## Chapter Nineteen

## DAWNING OF A NEW DAY

December 2, 1982. Christmas season is approaching. Dispositions change from sour to cheerful, the stores are decorated with Christmas trappings and the entire atmosphere is charged with expectancy. But there are no festive feelings in the hearts of my children, my sisters nor myself. Today is departure day. I have lived through many difficult days in my twenty-five years, but today is the worst one I will have to endure. My girls are glued to my side refusing to be separated from me. My sisters will take them to their respective places from the airport. Everyone gathers to help us deal with the changes. The bags are deposited into the car trunk and we're loaded into two cars for the sad trip to the airport. My children ride with me crying at the impending separation. They cling to each other knowing that in a couple hours not only are they going to lose their mother they will also be losing each other. How their young hearts ache, their lives have been shattered to pieces, they will no longer have each other to talk or play with, and worst of all, no mommy to love and care for them. To make matters worse I have no idea when we will be reunited. My poor children, how are they going to endure their losses? Everyone dear to them has disappeared from their lives.

At the airport they become inconsolable almost to the point of hysteria. My only choices are to get on the plane, or turn around and return from whence we came. Somehow I have a feeling that we will not be welcomed back in Uncle Duke's home. He had gotten tired of us. With super human strength we manage to dry our eyes, remove the bags from the trunk of the car, and follow the signs leading to Air Canada. My family enters the airport venturing as far as security allows. We spend more tearful minutes in long hugs and wet kisses.

# The Odyssey of Survival

With no more time to spare I say a final goodbye and turn and walk away from my children.

With red swollen eyes, and a heart about to burst, I turn to give a final wave, blowing kisses and mouthing I love you. Drying the tears from my eyes, I head for the terminal. The passengers are being boarded so there is no more time to procrastinate. The die has been cast.

Boarding an airplane in Jamaica requires the passengers to exit the building walk onto the tarmac then climb on board. The good thing about this is that loved ones have a final opportunity to watch you board the plane from the waving gallery. You can take an additional minute to turn around waving until you are swallowed up by the confines of the plane. As I approach the door of the plane my family shouts my name. I turn around and stand there waving for a minute while others push past me. I find my seat. Thank God I have the window. Gazing out the window at my children requires all my effort to keep from screaming. Panic rises up in my throat.

*"What have I done? This was a bad decision. Who is going to care for my children? No one can love them as dearly as I do. Who is going to tuck them in at night, comb their hair, and make their favorite meals?"* When am I going to see my children again?

*Oh my God help me. I have abandoned my children. I can't do this; I have to go to them. I know they're crying. I can hear them calling my name. I have to go."*

I have to get off the plane; I can't go through with this. Nausea rises up in the back of my throat threatening to spill out onto the person sitting next to me. Swallowing heavily I turn to the person in the next seat.

"Excuse me I need to get off the plane. My children need me."

I gather my purse and hand luggage together while attempting to unbuckle the seat belt. With a look of pure pity my seating companion says at me.

"Is this your first time leaving the Island?'

"No but this time is different." I stammer.

'Are you leaving family behind?"

"My two daughters, sisters and brothers."

"How long will you be gone?"

"I don't know. I miss them so much I want to go back, but there is nothing to go back to, this is an opportunity to help them but I don't want to leave them."

"Don't worry, they'll be fine. Many of us have had to leave our children behind at first but it will all work out in the end, you'll see. Just relax and enjoy the trip. You are going to provide a better life for them, they'll appreciate this later, and you'll be glad you were strong enough to do what is best for them now."

Enjoy the trip. Is she crazy? My only enjoyment is my children in my arms and now they were standing on a waving gallery weeping for me. Waves of emotions wash over me. I want to scream my head off but the situation allows no such display. In an attempt to control myself I press my face into the window trying to catch the last glimpse of my family while hiding my tears from the eyes of the passengers.

As the door closes and the wheels begin moving I watch in desperation as my children and family wave the plane out of sight. I know they are hurting and my children are crying their hearts out. I know they want their mummy back. I feel like a traitor, as if I had betrayed them. Silently I beg God to take care of them. This has to be done. I have to provide a better life for them. I'll get a job, send money back to care for them and as soon as possible bring them to Canada to join me. My other sisters have done it, now it's my turn to do it for my children. These thoughts help me to retain my sanity. This is for my children; I will do anything for them. This separation will not be for long. By the grace of God, we'll be back together soon.

My mother has not been told about my departure from Jamaica and that's the way I want it to be. I have not spoken to her since that fateful day and have no intentions of doing so.

New hatred rises up in me for her. It's her fault that I am in this situation. She is responsible for displacing us to the point of dissolution. I don't want to leave my children; they need me to protect them from the likes of Uncle Duke and their grandmother. Fresh tears course down my cheeks. A sob escapes my lips and my hand covers my mouth. Unable to conceal it my inner agony turns into soul racking sobs. A piece of tissue is handed to me, but it's not enough to stem the torrent of tears. My heart has been broken into a million pieces and scattered over the Caribbean Sea as the nose of the airplane lifted into the sky taking me thousands of miles from my two precious little daughters.

When will I see my children again?

"Oh Dear God I love my children more than life itself. Please watch over them and keep them safe. They are very precious to me, they are all I have. You gave them to me for a reason and I have to provide for them. So far I have done a lousy job, now they have been left behind in the hands of strangers. I miss them. They are going to suffer and cry for me but I must do this so I can provide for them. Please allow them to be properly cared for and keep them from harm and danger. Open a way for me in Canada and make it possible for us to be reunited in the very near future. Amen."

"Fear not for I am with you; do not be dismayed; for I am your God. I will strengthen and harden you to difficulties, yes, I will help you; yes I will hold you up and retain you with my right hand of righteousness and justice."
Isaiah 41: 10 (AKJV)


"Have faith in God because he loves and cares for you.
Have faith in God, he will help, strengthen, provide and keep you.
Have faith in God there is nothing he cannot do
Have faith in God he will see you through
Have faith, dear friends in GOD."

***Life Question:*** When life throws you lemons make lemonade. My lemons were poisonous. Leaving my children behind was the most horrific thing I had ever done, but there was no other way. Or was there? Is it possible that we could have survived without the agony of separation? Will my children understand and forgive me for leaving them or will they become bitter and grow to hate me? There are no guarantees for my future. What on earth is going to become of us? What would you have done?

***Answer:***

***What's next?*** *'The Long Wandering', coming fall of 2017. The Long Wandering completes the journey of The Odyssey of Survival, giving hope to the hopeless and help to the helpless. Visit my website for more information on how you can stay informed and connected. www.revampmylifeministries.com*

# The Odyssey of Survival

# The Odyssey of Survival

www.ingramcontent.com/pod-product-compliance
Lightning Source LLC
LaVergne TN
LVHW051547070426
835507LV00021B/2447